SALES MANAGER'S PROBLEM-SOLVER

SALES MANAGER'S PROBLEM-SOLVER

LEON A. WORTMAN

A Ronald Press Publication

JOHN WILEY & SONS

New York   Chichester   Brisbane   Toronto   Singapore

Library of Congress Cataloging in Publication Data:

Wortman, Leon A.
    How successful sales managers solve sales people problems.

    "A Ronald Press publication."
    1. Sales management—Psychological aspects.
    2. Sales personnel.   I. Title.

HF5438.4.W66 1982   658.3'044   82-16030
ISBN 0-471-09775-6

Printed in the United States of America

10   9   8   7   6   5   4   3   2   1

To Dorothy

PREFACE

People come in many more varieties than are found in any catalog of products or services. At some point(s) in my career in selling and in managing those who sell, I have encountered, worked with, worked for (and some might claim worked "against") at least one of each of the types of people described in this book. I admit I rarely enjoyed the problemsome sales person; that is to say, I did not always enjoy having to "work things out." The temptation to fall back on the power of rank is great. After all, it is I not they who have the manager's title! The use of rank is sometimes effective, but only when appropriate to the situation (such as a rapid, one-shot action that demands the most immediate action, with no time for in-depth discussion).

I hereby acknowledge, for the benefit of those who have waited all these years to hear me admit it, that I have not always been right. Who is always right? I am not certain, now, that a compliment was intended when it was said about me: "He may not always be right, but he's always the manager." I may never know the real meaning of this statement, as it applied to me.

Being a candid person, those for whom I worked (or to whom I was accountable) over the past years have already heard from me privately as to exactly what I thought of each of them as my boss. If any of them are still not sure or may still be wondering about what I meant when I said "You really are something," I will be glad to accept their invitations to lunch, cocktails or dinner (on their expense accounts) for a reappraisal. For those who do not wonder but know exactly what I meant, I will pick up the tab.

I would especially like to acknowledge Bob Johnston's contributions to my skills development, at Ampex and Dictaphone, in people-problem solving. He and I didn't always agree. He was usually more accurate than I was in an evaluation of the situation and the people. However, I believe I was more accurate in the types of solutions I proposed after we had arrived at consensus concerning a sales-person problem. Two heads were better than one, and I learned much from Bob.

I have tried very hard to be charitable about some of the companies I have worked for as a consultant or as an employee/manager. I am afraid I do not always feel charitable and must, from this point forward, omit all company names. Permit me the observation that company size has something to do with it. The bigger the company, the more concerned and insecure the managers are. They would most often rather fight in the political arena of the corporation than correct their own people-problems. Perhaps, the theory and the practice are that they can always find a scapegoat among their subordinates for any falldown in performance. It really is much harder to solve a people-problem than it is to just fire the offender as a way out of the difficulty. Thus, by summarily "solving" the immediate problem (getting rid of the trouble-maker), they can return their undivided attention to the game called "Up Your Ladder."

Bob Johnston was a person who could have been enormously successful as a political fighter. However, he preferred to try to win at the game without sacrificing his idealistic view of people. How did he make out? I had the pleasure of going to his "retirement" party—voluntary retirement, I assure you—when a financial investment he had made paid off. I believe that if he had been a political infighter, the corporation for which he worked would have made him the chief honcho and, as a result, it might have become profitable and still be alive today. A sad ending for the corporation, but a happy ending for Bob. He still lives in Palo Alto and works hard every day—planning his next fishing, hunting, or backpacking trip. Those who opposed him are also working hard every day—at survival!

LEON A. WORTMAN

September 1982
Palo Alto, California

CONTENTS

SALES MANAGER'S PROBLEM-SOLVER

Introduction

You are about to meet a lot of interesting people. You've probably met and worked with most of them before. In fact, some of them might even be working with or for you at this very moment. Furthermore, you could be one of the dozen or so people described in this book. You will enjoy meeting them. Though some may be familiar faces, you will see them in a special light and in an environment that bares all, and bars all efforts to conceal their most true feelings.

This is a workbook. It is intended for sales people, for those who already have the job function of sales manager or sales supervisor, for those who aspire to become leaders and managers of other sales people, and for those working in the "front lines" in eyeball-to-eyeball contact on a daily basis.

You may choose to skim this book, hopping randomly from chapter to chapter or scanning its contents sequentially. The way the material is presented enables you to pick and choose the chapters you wish to read at random, without the slightest loss in value.

You can get more out of this book than you put into it, I assure you. How much you "put into it" is entirely up to you. Therefore, you, not I, control how much you "get out of it." The same is true of managing sales people. What you give is related to what you get!

Being a manager is a difficult task. Being a leader of others is always a tough assignment. Too few of us know how to lead effectively. The dictum for the unskilled manager usually is "when all else fails, use your authority" (usually meaning "use your rank"). But there are several kinds of authority, two of which are of special value to the effective manager. One is the kind that depends entirely on power, the rank that is implied with the title "manager." The other kind is dependent upon *knowledge* and *skill*. The prudent manager recognizes that both kinds of authority are inherent in the title. "When" and "how" he applies his authority, and the appropriateness of his choice of the two kinds of authority relevant to the specific situation, are among the determinants of his true and long-term effectiveness as a manager.

What is a "manager"? You may be as tired of reading answers to this question as I am of being asked for a definition. Definitions range from the statistical/numerical: any person who has two or more persons reporting directly to him; to the pragmatic: any person who performs tasks through the work efforts of others; to the dictionary-type definition: to handle or direct with a degree of skill or address, as (a) to make and keep submissive, (b) to treat with care, (c) to alter by manipulation, (d) to direct or carry on business or affairs, (e) to achieve one's purpose.

No doubt, each is correct at some point in time and under certain conditions. However, the definition is not as important as the practice. So, we leave the defining of the word "manager" to the semanticists and move on to the pragmatics of being effective in the function of working with people—*sales people* who report to you, basically because that's the way the organization chart ranks you in the hierarchy, and who look to you for guidance, appraisal, and approval, because your methods are effective and your sales people know and like them.

The sales people you will meet in this book are, without exception, high achievers. We assume you, too, are a high achiever, a person with high self-expectations. You may be a sales manager now or are working toward this career objective. You are interested in learning how to be "good" (alternative word for "effective") at your chosen profession. One of the ways to learn is by reading, thereby reducing the probability for error. Another way is to learn by doing, also called "learning by trial and error." (Usually, your error and the trials of others.) We can't quarrel with the combination of "reading" and "doing." A foundation of book-learning never hurt anyone, some wise person observed.

This book requires *involvement* on your part. Make a game of it. Enjoy it. You will be presented with situations taken from the lives of sales managers and sales people. Each chapter presents you with a set of human circumstances that are affecting the ability of a high-achieving sales person, or a group of sales people, to perform at maximum potential. Your own productivity, which is the aggregate of the individual performances of your sales people, is beginning to hurt. The 80/20 rule that says that 80% of the results are produced by 20% of your people tells you, in reverse English, that you must devote 80% of your energies to 20% of your people.

You are about to meet such familiar people as the sales person who won't get his call and sales reports done on time (when *you* need them), the one who won't plan ahead but prefers to "fly by the seat of his pants," and the one who fights every effort you make to change any thing or any procedure. There is the district manager who strangles his people with a morass of rules and regulations. You will encounter the sales person who constantly repeats his mistakes and never seems to learn from them. You'll love or hate the one who is inflexible and can't see things any way but his way. Then there are others: the one who confuses everybody because of poor communications skills (but he sure can close a sale), the malcontent, the underpaid type (are the complaints about money just that or do they conceal more deeply seated problems), and those who are very valuable though troublesome people.

One more note before we begin. It is quite awkward to constantly refer to "he/she," "his/hers," and "him/her." It is simply more convenient to use one form of reference such as "he." But, when we say "he," "his," "him," we also mean "she, "hers," and "her." No preference, special recognition, or discrimination by gender is intended or implied; none should be inferred. In this book, and in keeping with growing actual practice, the term "sales man" is totally interchangeable with "sales woman." Each one individually is a "sales person." Both together are "sales people."

Come on in. The reading's fine.

1 TRY THIS FOR AN "OPENER"

... To Good Sales Management

"What common denominators identify good managers?" That popular question is often asked and discussed by teachers and students of management techniques and by those who have the word "manager" built into their titles. Are there any denominators that are "common" to good managers? And just what is a "good" manager?

These questions may strike you as being purely theoretical and abstract, hardly worth the time it could take away from really getting things done. However, despite such a viewpoint (if this is indeed your viewpoint), the questions persist and discussion continues.

IDENTIFICATION OF A GOOD MANAGER

In order to determine whether or not there are any common denominators we must determine what identifies a *good manager*. Let's develop some definitions, in a question-and-answer format, that deal with the real world in which sales managers live and work:

Q: Is the sales manager's work objective to be *popular* among his sales people?

A: It doesn't hurt one bit to be popular with one's subordinates. If this is the sales manager's prime objective and if he is indeed popular, he may be declared, in this sense, to be a good manager because he is meeting his personal objective. (However, bear in mind that his supervisor and his company may have a different set of priorities concerning objectives.)

Q: Is the sales manager's work objective to develop a definitive sales plan, to open a sales territory, to deliver a quantity of orders for products or services measured in units or dollars?

A: This is usually the written or stated objective for the sales manager, generally described as a *quota system*. If the sales manager makes or exceeds his quota, he is usually thought to be a good or even top manager.

Q: Can a sales manager become a good or top manager without actually being popular?

A: It's been done, provided the alternative to popularity is not unpopularity. In direct response, it is quite possible for any manager to be a good or top manager without being popular. This is, for many, a difficult concept to grasp (i.e., being good, top, or effective without being popular). Many sales managers who succeed in making or exceeding quota are not necessarily well-liked by their sales people; however, they invariably have gained the respect of their sales people as being very professional sales managers. These professional sales managers develop their authority and influence entirely on the basis of their knowledge of sales techniques and of their sales people and their motivational needs. Also, they have the ability to share and transfer this valuable knowledge to their subordinates. They do not depend on authority based on titular rank within the organization.

Q: Doesn't this leave the sales manager with only two choices: (1) be effective or (2) be popular?

A: On the surface it might appear that these are the limited options open to the sales manager. However, the real "choices" are not really "options." The successful sales manager must be effective, that is to say he must *make or exceed quota,* and at the same time must control his *unpopularity* and be less concerned with his *popularity.*

Q: Are we going around in a big circle? Are we getting all wrapped up in a play on words?

A: The question of popularity is so often raised that it has to be dealt with in both the semantic and pragmatic senses. Why? Because when one believes that popularity is all-important, the implication and inference are that to be less-than-popular can cause certain failure! Unpopularity, one may be led to believe, must be avoided at all costs! The sales manager who adheres rigidly to this set of values is in serious danger of following a path that may lead to self-destruction, as far as "effectiveness" is concerned.

The choice may have to be made—be *effective* or be *popular.* Few can succeed at being both. The trouble is too few sales managers know how to be effective without expending lots of time and energy on building their personal popularity levels. Too often, these sales managers become frustrated in their efforts to be effective in quota attainment. They say, "Gee, I bust my back to treat my sales people right. I do this and that for them. And what do I get for it? Nothing! No loyalty! No support!"

Many sales managers were, first of all, superior salespeople. Unfortunately, when they become managers of other sales people, they fail to recognize that they are no longer expected to make or close the "sale," except, of course, when the "power" of the office of the sales manager is required, or the manager is given or takes upon himself the responsibility for servicing specific accounts or classes of accounts. Many fail to realistically recognize that they must now *make or exceed quota* primarily through the efforts of others—their subordinate salespeople. Too often they lose touch with the fact that all their sales people are just that—*people!*

And that is what this book is all about, sales managers, sales people, and their problems.

In order to be successful, the sales manager must learn to deal with *people* as well as he does with *things*. Every single day, the sales manager actively copes with "thing-problems" and with "people-problems." In all probability, the sales manager proved his skills in dealing with thing-problems when he was a sales person. It is very probable he was promoted or moved into sales management because he had great skills in solving this type of problem. But, people-problems can prove to be something else! They *are* something else—quite different from thing-problems!

Good managers do have a common denominator. They are experts at recognizing people-problems. More important, they are expert at solving these problems. When and if they are also popular, is usually because of their ability to solve these problems in such a way that they are able to satisfy the needs and wants of the individual sales person, their own needs, and those of the company. They make sure *nobody loses!*

QUANTIFICATION AND QUALIFICATION

As a sales manager, you deal every day with quantities, with performances that are measured in finitely quantified sets of information. You may quantify the performance of a product or of a service in units or dollars delivered, usually against some predetermined goal or quota for a specified time period. The units or dollars delivered are translated into terms of (1) product performance in sales, and (2) performance of the sales people who brought in the orders. A sales person and a product both "perform well" when the units are high relative to goal or quota. The sales people who produce, who bring in the orders in quantities that meet or surpass the assigned quotas are considered high achievers. Throughout this book we will be dealing with sales people who are high achievers, productive in units or dollars relative to quotas or assignments.

Perhaps you are or have been a high achiever. It is entirely possible this is one of the reasons you are now a sales manager, or have a high probability of becoming a sales manager. Past, present, or future, during your career in sales and in sales management you have had, are having, or will have at any moment a personal experience with a high achiever who has stopped "achieving," or who has become a major source of difficulty, an irritant, a creator of conflict and dissension. Once one of your favorite and most admired sales people, he is rapidly becoming one of your most significant distractions—a people-problem! He puts you to tests that you feel you don't need, certainly don't want, but can't ignore. And no one but you is expected to solve the problem.

Your title, duties, and accountabilities as sales manager are all-inclusive. They relate to the management of products, services, and people. Of course, you are involved in sales, bringing in orders and bookings that can be converted to deliveries and shipments. These become measurements of the merits of individual and group performance, billings and invoices that produce the cash flow from which salaries, bonuses, and commissions are paid and profits generated. It has not been demonstrably proven, except in science fiction, that products or services can emulate human feelings.

"What you see is what you get" may be an oversimplification as far as some high-technology products are concerned; however, when a product or a service fails who do you call for? Certainly not a spiritual leader, or a psychologist. You call for a person with special *product-related* technical skills— not a *people-oriented* specialist. The people-oriented specialist deals with purely *qualitative* factors—*people*—and there is probably no technology, product, or service as complex as people.

As a manager of sales, you must have technical skills in selling, product and market knowledge, knowledge of the technological environment in which your product or service is designed to compete, and other facts that can be published in a catalog or specification sheet. But what we will deal with in this book are the extraordinary skills every sales manager must have that go beyond the selling of products and services. As a manager of sales, you must be highly skilled in the management of people, especially the most complex types of people (yes, people do come in various degrees or levels of complexity). And, as you have probably already learned, the high achievers among your sales people are the most complex of all.

It is a mixed "blessing" to have high achievers among your sales people. The good news is obvious—they bring in the business and keep the customers coming back for more. The bad news comes shortly thereafter; the high achievers can generate more internal, hard-to-handle conflicts than those who do not achieve at the same levels.

When a high-achieving sales person becomes "defective" or doesn't meet the specifications you have established or that he established through previous examples of his own performance capabilities, you can't call in the engineering department for help. They can't change components or re-design the person. You can't call in the manufacturing department and ask them to have quality control take a look. The shipping department can't reconfigure the container. None of the finance department's accounting rules will have the desired long-term effect on the quality of the person.

One may threaten, cajole, and implore the person to reach out and up to greater heights and intensified effort. One can shout "get off my back please," "get that chip off your shoulder, buddy," and other clichés from our childhood. One may make promises (some of which are intended to be kept but which often turn out to be "unkeepable") of great financial or material rewards; but some, probably most, will fall flat and will not achieve the desired result. The carrot you dangle may turn out to be your own self-threatening Sword of Damocles.

Yes, managing products can be reduced to documentation, specifications, diagrams, schematics, drawings, and blueprints. Once the configuration, design, specifications, and tolerances are established, when everything has been quantified, the product either has integrity or it doesn't—black and white, virtually. To a large degree, changes in design, components, and tolerances will produce highly predictable results. Computers can do the calculations in microseconds and hand you a printout in minutes that reliably forecasts the future for the hardware's performance.

No doubt, in the cellars and attics of think-tanks and non-profit organizations engaged in advanced studies of human beings, work is being done in the science of forecasting human responses or reactions to given sets of conditions and environments. Especially vital is the development of the predictability of the responses of people interacting with other people. At this point in time, this ability to predict the behavior of people is more *art* than *science.* But you know this, don't you? You've learned this already. What can we do about it? A whole lot!

THEORY SUPPORTS PRACTICE

Most sales managers have learned to manage the hard way, by doing. Often, unfortunately, there is no other "school" than the school of "hard knocks" available to the person whose career ambitions are to become a sales manager or to one who already holds the title and the accountability. Also, too often, the hard knocks are those received by the manager's subordinates as a result of his learning curve or of his inadequacies as a manager of people. Great with things, terrible with people!

There is at least one theory, but often there are several theories to support any practice. The practice of good sales management demands a solid and sturdy foundation in the theories of human behavior. Intuition and "gut feel," when they work in one's favor, are fine things to have and to exercise. But, they may not prove to be dependable management tools. "Trying things on for size" may not be a prerogative of a sales manager when it comes to managing people. You may sell samples of a product to a select variety of customers or markets to determine what promotions or mixes are effective. You may not tamper with the lives of people, testing your own favorite ideas and schemes in an effort to determine "what turns them on." The test-market approach does not guarantee product-marketing success but, because it is usually based on a mixture of marketing theory that is supported by practice, it certainly reduces the risk elements.

There are many theories of human behavior. These are referred to collectively as the *behavioral sciences.* A sound knowledge of these theories and the sets of logic under which they were formed is essential to effective management. Because they are continuously exposed to and involved in situations that demand interaction with others, sales people are especially vulnerable to people-problems. And, by correlation, the manager of sales people comprehends the complexity of the sales person's needs and the individual motivational forces that are in play.

The sales manager is empathetic and sympathetic. By this we do not mean to imply he is at all tolerant of foreign or negative behavior. We do mean that he is quick to recognize a people-problem among his sales people. He is able to recognize the problem rapidly, analyze it accurately and develop the appropriate responses that will correct the situation before it becomes magnified out of control. If, as can happen to a sales manager on whom many demands are placed, the situation is already on the brink of being out of control, the effective sales manager is able to call upon his knowledge of the theories of human behavior. He combines this knowledge with his experience to bring order back, avoid chaos, and create a positive environment in which all can find satisfaction.

Getting Down to Cases

In the chapters which follow we present a group of situations that are true-to-life case studies in people-problem solving. Each of the studies presents a conflict, a serious disagreement, or a potential conflict that must be dealt with before it has a negative effect on anyone's performance. The conflict, active or potential, is between the sales manager and one of the sales people, or with one of the supervisors in the manager's group. Each chapter offers the reader a key to the successful management of sales people problems.

We will not become involved with the classic how-to-sell, how-to-overcome-objections, how-to-turn-a-no-into-a-yes, make-a-million-dollars, or other clichés. The learning and application of these techniques are not the purpose of this book.

From this point on *you* are the sales manager. The problems and conflicts you will encounter in each of the chapters are extremely important to your own effectiveness, the group's performance and, possibly, to your reputation as a manager. You can't ignore them. The problems and conflicts just won't go away. They cannot be passed along to someone else to handle. The "buck stops at your place!"

It doesn't matter one bit what kind of product or service your company delivers or the group sells. It doesn't matter what the gender, race, color, creed, religion, or nationality of your sales people may be. The conflicts you will be dealing with in this book are universal among sales managers and sales people.

Did you inherit the problem? It doesn't matter. It's yours now! No alibis allowed. Sure, your predecessor may have left a mess behind as he moved on, up, or out of the company. No use claiming "it happened on his watch!" It's your "watch" now and you have no choice but to find a positive solution and create a "happy ending" for each of the conflicts; you own the problem now!

A "positive solution and a happy ending" is one in which there are *no losers* and one which promises a *long-term benefit* to all participants. Some of the problems might be quickly resolved by firing the person who you feel is the cause of the conflict. However, there could very well be some serious and undesirable side effects. The act of firing someone has hazards that bear a strong resemblance to those formidable days in classical history when the bearer of bad news was executed. "You are *fired*" is pretty bad news to deliver.

TOO GOOD TO FIRE, TOO HARD TO KEEP

Let's assume the sales person or subordinate manager to whom you refer as my "problem child" is one of the most productive people in your group, dependably closing the tough ones and great at opening new accounts. Losing this particular person's technical skills could and probably would have a very noticeable effect on your team's aggregate statistical performance. As a sales person, this individual is beyond challenge. You are quite aware of the fact that if you were to fire this person, your competition would literally snap him right up. You don't want or need the added burden of selling against this high achiever as a member of your competition's sales force.

You wish, however, that the headaches didn't have to come with the benefits. You could put your time to much better use than thinking about and becoming uptight about this problem child. Unfortunately, the responsibility for dealing with such situations comes with the sales manager's territory. No, you do not want to fire this person. You do want to solve the problem and retain the high productivity, the quota-busting capabilities of the sales group.

Let's not consider any other way through this situation than to work it out in a way that neither you nor the problem child loses. It can be done. It *must* be done. It is being done all the time by successful sales managers. In fact, in not one of the situations presented in the succeeding chapters of this book is *firing* the problem generator one of your desirable options.

Most of the chapters in this book are self-contained studies. Each "study" is dedicated to a typical, important, and complex problem that every sales manager or supervisor has to deal with successfully. Each case-study chapter begins with a comprehensive statement and description of the nature of the situation and of the personalities that are involved. After each statement and description you are offered a choice of several possible solutions or options. Any one of them may appear to be okay and workable. In fact, many of them will work just fine, but only for the short term. This means the problem will very likely recur, returning to bedevil you more than ever before. It will not have been *resolved*, but merely driven undergound, disguised, or dressed up with wishful thinking and the hope that it will go away.

You must, for the sake of everyone involved and for the good of the company, select the option which offers the greatest assurance for long-term success—the one option that is most likely to produce the desired "happy ending." In each case, one of the options offered is better than the others; it will take careful thought on your part to recognize the one option which is best.

You do not have to start with the next chapter. You can start with any chapter and move randomly throughout the book. Each case study can stand on its own. If one of the situations "strikes" a responsive chord or seems to resemble an immediate situation, start with that one. Wherever you start, read each of the statements and descriptions carefully.

One or more may very well fit a situation or problem you are trying to resolve at this moment (difficult, isn't it?), or one that you've had in the past (how well did it work out?), or may run into in the very near future (watch it!).

Each of the problem persons described is subordinate to you in the organizational hierarchy. This person might be one of your managers (national, regional, district, or branch) or strictly at a line level. He reports directly to you.

The problem is quite serious. You can't ignore it any longer. You'd like to "let nature take its course," but you know the unpredictability and perversity of "mother nature." The time has come when you have to take action! In fact, it is very prudent to discuss the situation with your own superior. But, again, as a professional manager you do not just want to report a problem to your superior in the organization. It is quite appropriate for him to expect you to propose a course of corrective action at the same time that you describe the existence of a significant problem within your group. Certainly, he will want to review with you each of the options you have examined. He will want to know why you rejected some of them and, especially, why the one you chose is most likely to bring about a long-term solution.

As you go through each of the situations and the options that are offered, use a sheet of scratch paper to note the following as an aid to your decision-making process:

1. The probable results of pursuing each of the options; describe the short- and the long-term benefits as you see them.

2. The option you believe you should pursue (with your superior's approval).

3. The reasons and logic that support your rejection of specific options.

4. The reasons and logic that support your choice of the specific option as the one most likely to achieve the desired result.

Out of fairness to yourself, do not read ahead of the problem or the options within the chapter on which you are working. After you have completed your notes, read the section, "Discussion of Options (Pro and Con)" that appears at the end of each chapter. Compare your notes with the recommendations and reasoning that are given. No option is entirely "wrong." We are dealing with *probabilities for long-term success.*

While this book deals in how to work with the highly pragmatic aspects of the management of sales people and people-problem solving, it would be pure fiction if it were not based on the theory or theories of human behavior. Therefore, you will be guided through a series of jargon-free presentations of these theories in the chapters that follow the individual case studies. You are urged to read each of the theories very carefully so you fully understand them. This will enable you to get the most out of the specific discussions and solutions of the people problems and problem solving that form the core and heart of this book. If you prefer, you may move directly to the chapters on theory, and then deal with the how-to examples and case studies.

Whether you start sequentially with the very next chapter or move randomly throughout the book, your reading, pondering and analyzing can dramatically improve your chances for a successful career in sales management and for earning the rich emotional and material rewards that lie beyond. This is a fact!

2 HOT-SHOT

He Thinks He's Ready for Promotion, but He's not, Really

Here's a winner! Just ask this sales person "Are you a winner?" The answer will most likely be "How did you know?" He really is an outstanding performer in sales. He *is a Hot-Shot!* Trouble is that, although he is always right at the top in productivity and always meeting or beating quota, he isn't quite the versatile individual he believes he is. Not quite.

IMMEDIATE PROMOTION REQUESTED

He thinks his time has come to be promoted to sales manager. He's not the least bit subtle about letting you—and everybody else—know that this is the way he feels. He's not kidding one bit. Hot-Shot honestly believes he is ready to take on the responsibility of managing the work of other sales people.

He doesn't mean he wants *your* job. But, the grapevine has it that a new slot will be opening in the near future for a district sales manager. Your Hot-Shot is making it quite clear that he expects to get the job. A crisis is coming because you cannot convince yourself that he is at all ready for this level of responsibility.

You have always rewarded and would like to continue to reward your sales people who turn in outstanding work. Whenever possible, you do openly demonstrate your appreciation for work that has been done well on behalf of the group and the company. This is your style. However, in the case of Hot-Shot you have some very strong doubts about his ability, or his willingness, to identify with the team—his peers in the sales department.

Hot-Shot strikes you clearly as a "soloist," a loner who doesn't fully recognize the contributions that are made by the other members of the sales group. Also, this time, the grapevine has it wrong. There is no district sales manager job opening planned for the near future.

No matter now. This is no time for philosopy. You have just received a letter from Hot-Shot. It is quite clear you have a crisis on your hands. As you have come to expect from your past experiences, Hot-Shot's letter is very direct:

> I have worked for this company as a sales man for the past two years. I have always made or beaten my quota, no matter how tough it was. I have built every one of my accounts to new high sales volumes, and opened more new accounts than anyone else in the sales department. My performance reviews have always rated me "excellent." You, your own boss, and others have often told me I am an exceptional sales man. I have no complaints about the money and the bonuses I have earned here. I am ready for a sales manager's job, the next one that opens up. If this company can't use my talents I will have only one choice to make. What do you say?

*   *   *

You have several rapid reactions to this one and it takes a great deal of self-control to keep your cool! This is not surprising. Nobody likes to be handed an ultimatum, and this letter sure sounds like one—*make me a manager, or else!*

What is he really saying to you? Does he believe the grapevine rumors about a new district sales manager job opening? Possibly. Or, is he quitting in his own "charming" way? Possibly. Either one of these possibilities is very awkward for you. Sometimes it is harder to find a good sales person than it is to find a profitable customer. No matter what the title may be, people who are as productive as Hot-Shot are rare indeed.

You sure would hate to have to tell your boss that you have to replace one of the best sales people you have. (The boss is always looking at the "bottom line," qualifying people according to their quantitative outputs. He doesn't have to put up with their idiosyncracies on a daily basis. He doesn't really want to hear about their personality quirks. Among other things, that's one of the reasons you are there.)

You are naturally somewhat concerned that the boss (and possibly others in the company) might interpret Hot-Shot's departure as your mistake. "Hot-Shot" is a nickname that is not generally used throughout the company, but only among those who work with him every day.

This all adds up to the fact you can no longer ignore the situation or postpone resolving this conflict, this nagging problem. Hot-Shot's letter is probably a good thing. You have cooled off and you accept the letter as a valuable catalyst for change—but change that you will *manage* and *control.* Your objective is quite clear now. The change, whatever its form, must be such that there are *no losers.* You will find a way to keep Hot-Shot on the job. But, not just on the job. You will keep him motivated to achieve so he remains a high producer. And, as a result, you will gain a new level of self-esteem and the respect of your superiors, peers, and subordinates as an exceptionally effective manager of sales people.

This situation, this conflict, this problem takes very careful thought and analysis. You give it all it requires and, without waiting too long, you narrow down the courses of action to four options. You believe that any one of the four will work. However, some may not have truly beneficial long-term effects; they are good, primarily, only for the short term. But the option you want, the option you must exercise is the one that holds the greatest promise for long-term benefits for all concerned—Hot-Shot, the company, the group, and, of course, your own career.

Your response must be made in the face of two very important restraints: (1) there are in truth no openings for a sales manager right now and it is not at all realistic to even attempt to name a date when an opening will actually occur, and, at least as important, (2) you honestly believe that Hot-Shot is not at all ready to perform as a manager of a group of sales people, despite his high, but unrealistic, self-esteem.

You are a team-player, and you very well know the benefits that are realized through team participation. You and your own boss have always operated this way. It is not your style, nor is it his expectation to ever hear you say that a very serious personality problem exists in the department—not without immediately hearing your detailed description of what you intend to do about it. You will do what you know he expects of you. You will communicate with him in detail. You will demonstrate your professionalism again. (Not that he has ever doubted it, but there is no harm at all in giving a demonstration once again.) As a result, your experience has proven repeatedly that you will gain his complete support for a positive recommendation for action.

Using your scratch-pad, you list the options that appear to be open, remembering that firing Hot-Shot is *not* one of them. You examine each of the options carefully, evaluating the *long-* and *short-term* effects each might have. You list your reasons for preferring one over the others. You recognize that, generally, any one of them will work with some degree of success. None can be called "wrong." But, you do have to select and propose one specific option that is best for all participants.

The next section of this chapter contains four courses of action—options that you will examine and from which you will make your choice. Which will you reject, accept and why?

THESE ARE YOUR OPTIONS

A.   Make a promise to Hot-Shot, one you mean to keep of course. Promise that he will get the first manager's spot that opens. You will personally see to this. You mean it. Ask him to "hold on!" A premium promotion will come along, and it's his when it does. This might also slow down his headlong rush to climb the managerial ladder. At least it will cool things down, keep him in the department, and take the pressure off.

B.   Heck, the budgt can probably stand a nice increase in Hot-Shot's base salary. You also have the special incentive budget for contingencies. Remember how often he has mentioned how much he'd like to go to that national convention? Tell him he and his wife are going—and the company is picking up the tab. This ought to calm him down by giving him some of the special recognition he obviously needs. It's one way of telling him you do appreciate the job he is doing in sales.

C.   On the other hand, no more fooling around with this guy. You will interpret his letter to you as a formal resignation. You are not *firing* him, just accepting his written *resignation*; just accepting his personal *challenge*. Once a manager gives into a subordinate's ultimatum he's done for. He loses all control of the group and ceases to be a *leader*. You've seen it happen to others and you are certainly not going to let it happen to you! No way. You can't afford to have anyone in the sales group get the impression that the way to get anything out of you is through pressure. You can't let anyone present an *ultimatum:* "Do it my way, *or else!*" After all, he started it. This is a perfect opportunity to reaffirm your position and set an example for appropriate behavior.

Promotions, in your group, go to those who have earned them and who are willing to do what the company expects of them. *Demands* just don't hack it! On the other side of the coin, however, you don't want any feelings floating around the company or the group that you are a very *rough* guy to work for. Therefore, anyone who wants to know why Hot-Shot left the company will learn that *he* resigned and you can honestly say: "I sure hated to lose the guy, but you know how these things happen.

D.   Well, no denying it, the guy is a Hot-Shot as a sales person. He's never had the opportunity to learn how to manage anyone else. Quite likely he doesn't really know what is involved in being a manager—all the administrative details and tasks that are not directly related to selling. His "bottom line" in sales, his effectiveness in the field would indicate he does a very good job of managing himself with customers. There's that old question coming back to haunt you: "Are managers *made* or are they *born to it?*" You don't have the answer to this one (who does?). But you are willing to believe that they can be *made,* because you've seen for yourself what specialized training and education can do for people who were not able to find the way to get ahead in their jobs.

Hot-Shot seems to have the primary requisites for career advancement: motivation, need, drive, energy, intelligence, and high self-expectations. You could help Hot-Shot plan and pursue a comprehensive training program that is specifically directed at developing managerial skills and savvy. Your thought is to tactfully, but very directly, describe to him all the things for which a manager is accountable. Most likely he doesn't really know, although he may *think* he knows.

You won't make any promises other than this: Should an

opening come along that matches his skills, his credentials as a top-producing salesman, combined with special managerial training, will certainly rank him among the candidates from which the final selection would be made. One more thing you feel you should point out to him. You do have an obligation to offer the same training program to all members of the sales group. In fact, some of the others in the group might very well be attending the same seminars and taking the same courses side-by-side with him. Even though not everybody wants to be a manager, good personnel practice requires that the same opportunities be offered to all people who are at the same level in the organization. This, too, is your style.

DISCUSSION OF OPTIONS (PRO AND CON)

A. Hot-Shot may take your promise as a very serious one. In fact, he may very well look at it as a *commitment* more than as a *promise.* The commitment he might choose to hear is *You are the next sales manager!* Suppose that, when the next open spot does come along, you realize that someone else in the group is actually better equipped for advancement into sales management than Hot-Shot is. Although you never did actually promise or commit the job to Hot-Shot (in your own mind, that is), he sincerely thinks he has your firm *promise* and that you *meant what you said.*

Now, if you selected Option A, you have an additional problem to cope with: *You didn't keep your word!* Most likely, Hot-Shot will resign on the spot in a high temper. He will feel you deceived him deliberately. If for no other reason than to save face and preserve his own ego-defense, he will be compelled to resign.

Suppose another set of circumstances related to the "promise" of a promotion should arise. Suppose he gets tired of waiting for the *next* sales manager job to open up. He could quietly start a search for a new job—possibly with one of your competitors. In the meantime, he may lose his motivation, his drive may weaken, his strong need to achieve (at least in your company's environment) may diminish, and his productivity will probably fall off. Furthermore, he may not continue to be innovative, will undoubtedly become negative about selling for the company and, especially, will be down on you. Everybody loses. No, you certainly do *not* have the best course of action in Option A.

B.   In some corners of the community this is referred to as "industrial bribery." Remember, Hot-Shot is hard to manage, a soloist. But, he is an intelligent and perceptive person with regard to his environment. He may not be very objective about himself as an individual (few of us are objective about ourselves), but he knows the score when his turn comes to bat.

He will surely recognize that your offer of a reward is a weakly disguised attempt to evade the issue—to "put him off." He could feel quite insulted by such a response to his letter. Read the letter again and you will see that he has no complaint about financial matters. *Money* is not the "root" of this conflict.

Hot-Shot has a need for a form of recognition that is quite different from the recognition that your offer attempts to provide. He needs the recognition of *status*—the form of recognition that comes with the title and responsibility of being a manager. He would like to hold this title in your company. But, if your company will not or cannot provide this, he will search elsewhere for it. And, based on his sales record, he will probably have little or no trouble finding a company that will take him on as a sales manager right from the beginning.

"It won't work out" you say. Well, it might not work out, neither for him nor for his new employer. But, the important point is that, once again, everybody loses. You don't want to have this kind of ending. It's not the "happy ending" you are searching for. Option B is clearly not the best way to go.

C.   Enough already! How much can anyone take of this

type of personality? Accept his *resignation letter* and face up to the hardships that will follow for a while. However, look at the other side of this fuzzy coin. He might just have the makings of a *good* sales manager. You don't really know one way or the other, do you? Sure he thinks he can do anything better than anyone else can. Maybe, just maybe, he isn't too far away from reality. What if one of your competitors discovers that he does have the real stuff out of which effective sales managers are made? You lose! Your company loses, too! Your superior, your peers, your subordinates—and your competitor who hires him—may not let you forget how you "let him get away."

There is still another factor here that must be taken into account. It is possible that others in the company (and the grapevine will tell the whole world) will read the incident as "Hot-Shot showed some ambition and he had to leave the company in order to get somewhere." Can't you hear it rumbling back down the grapevine—"maybe we didn't like working with Hot-Shot, but guess you have to be careful around here and don't step outside your boundaries, keep your place, the boss might feel threatened by you and *zap!*"

Option C? There must be, and there is, a better resolution available to you.

D.   Hot-Shot never said he wanted to run the company, to be president or chairman of the board. He never even indicated he wanted *your* job. What he did express was a personal need for recognition that had to be satisfied, and the sooner the better. But, notice he never gave a deadline in his letter. Yes, he did sound a bit impatient. There is a strong tone of "ultimatum." But he did not say "right away, or else." Of course, he's hot to trot on a new track.

True, he might have been a bit more delicate and diplomatic in the way he tried to find out whether or not he has a future with the company. You know he is a very direct person. That's not necessarily bad or evil. You know he is not famous for being subtle with you. Doesn't this also indicate he has always been honest and wide open with you? Isn't this good?

Under Option D you propose to discuss the situation with Hot-Shot in a "neutral arena." A neutral arena is a non-threatening meeting place. Although not the perfect location, it could be in your office—with both of you sitting on the same side of the desk, *not* with him in front and you in that big chair, that symbol of power behind your desk. You will quite calmly and professionally discuss these facts concerning company policy, your practice in relation to these policies, and his needs:

1. When an opening occurs that represents advancement to a higher grade, it is your style and company policy to announce it to the entire group of potentially eligible employees so each may have an equal opportunity to express interest in the opening. (This is one of the few things you like concerning government regulation and laws about discrimination.) Therefore, you cannot *promise* him the next sales manager's job that comes along.

2. You will put to rest or support the grapevine rumors with facts about a new opening coming along for a district sales manager.

3. Should an opening occur, the selection from among the eligible candidates will be made by an executive "jury" who will do it through the consensus process. The jury will consist of representatives from management, including your own supervisor, the personnel department, and you.

4. Elements that will influence the decision will, no doubt, consist of: the individual's performance or quantified track-record; a qualitative evaluation of the candidate's ability to interact with his peers and his superiors; his apparent (although not yet proven) ca-

pabilities as a manager; his abilities as a communicator, delegator, and team player; and a demonstrated effort at self-improvement through the constructive use of his time outside the company attending seminars, workshops, and taking related home-study or night-school courses.

It is abundantly clear that Hot-Shot will probably rank highest in "quantified track record" and near the bottom in peer acceptance and teamwork. But, because of his high self-expectations, drive, productivity, intelligence, and willingness to work hard, you want to and will help him move in a positive direction that will enable him to satisfy his needs as well as those of the company. You will *work* with him.

Together you will call on the personnel department and, if the company structure supports such a function, the training director. You will ask them to design and put into action a manager-skills development program. There are many such resources available at colleges, universities, and private schools. Numerous seminars and workshops lasting from one day to several weeks are offered by many training specialists.

You and Hot-Shot will set up a number of benchmarks and time intervals when you, personnel, and the training director will meet with him to review his progress. Again, you will make him aware of the fact that the same benefits must be offered to others who want to qualify for the next sales manager's opening.

Competition won't frighten Hot-Shot! In fact, he probably thrives on competition. His reaction will most likely be positive. He will see a specific direction of movement that will help him satisfy his needs. He will remain turned on, highly motivated, and productive.

Whether he knows it or not, he will be undergoing a behavior modification program, and that is not easy. With your help and the company's support, he has a good chance of doing it and making it work. If he succeeds, you and the company will enjoy the benefits of his renewed energies and improved personality. Not to be overlooked, your reputation will be enhanced as a manager who helps his sales people advance in their careers—surely an asset to the company's growth.

This sounds like *everybody wins.* You will have no difficulty gaining your supervisor's support for Option D.

3 JOE GUERILLA

Your "Underground" Competition

Everybody knows *you* are the sales manager, the person from whom all members of the sales group take their orders. *You* are accountable for the group's performance. Nobody but *you* gives the orders around here!

Well, isn't that the way it's supposed to be? People cannot serve two masters. There can and must be only one leader. You've been a leader for quite some time. You weren't born yesterday, nor did you become a sales manager just yesterday. You know the ropes. You have the knowledge and skills that are equal to anyone's in the company, as far as managing the sales group is concerned.

FOLLOW THE LEADER

So, what's the gripe? Your gripe? Well, you have the feeling that many of your instructions to your sales people are not being followed. In fact, it seems many of your most important instructions are being ignored or quite noticeably modified. It is happening too often—much too often to be coincidence or oversight.

There is another strange phenomenon that you can't help but notice, and it is quite disturbing. When your people take action, supposedly in response to your orders, there is a certain "camaraderie," a togetherness and cohesion that would be something great *under other circumstnaces.* Whoever heard of a sales manager complaining about camaraderie, togetherness, and cohesion in his department? The strange phenomenon is that the spirit of "marching along together" that you observe is all too often in a direction that bears little, if any, resemblance to the orders or instructions you gave on how a task should be performed. Before paranoia sets in, you sit down and try to figure out just what is happening here.

It's not too hard to figure out, really. The group, *your* sales people are listening to somebody else! Of course! That's it—right out of the textbooks on management!

You are the *formal leader* of the group. But, an *informal leader* has emerged and, deliberately or otherwise, he or she is now more dominant, playing a more influential role in leadership than you are! And, what's more, you think you know exactly who this informal leader is—this *Joe Guerilla!* He's one of your top salesmen—and he's behaving like an underground rebel, a guerilla fighter, a gang leader! He's working (so it seems in the heat of this discovery) to *undermine you*—and you thought he was your buddy. He was your "pet" and you were his favorite "teacher."

What happened? Why did he emerge as the informal leader of the group? Why does the group *need* an informal leader? Was it something you did or something you didn't do when you should have?

Clearly, the situation has to be brought back under proper control—your control. If you have made some sort of error it will obviously have to be corrected. But, the first order of importance is the relationship between you (the formal leader), and Joe Guerilla (the informal leader).

You have several options or courses of action you can

follow. One of them offers the best long-term benefits for the group, the company, and you. There's pressure on you in the short term to make your quota of orders (i.e., the group's quota). You've been seeing a serious falldown in general performance and you know by now that cajoling, threatening, and promising rewards haven't been working the way they used to. You must regain the support of the group. You recognize you can't do it without Joe Guerilla. He has always been your most productive sales person.

You have no intention of firing him. You will turn the situation around without losing this valuable member of your sales group. Perhaps, when we explore your options we will learn more about the environment that caused an informal leader to emerge; what enables him to continue his apparent domination of the group; what constructive actions will restore the hierarchy to its formal structure; and what you, the formal leader, can do to prevent recurrences.

THESE ARE YOUR OPTIONS

A.   It's time to bring the group together for a solid discussion of "who's who" and "what's what" around here. Of course, Joe Guerilla will be included in the meeting. Tempers, including yours, may be running high and hot, so you will take extra care in the way you handle yourself and everyone else throughout the entire meeting. The objective of the meeting is to remind your subordinates who the formal leader is. Of course, they know *you* are the boss; but, it appears that some may have forgotten this simple fact. Without threatening any one person, you will point out that you are aware that some of your instructions are not being followed and this kind of resistance must be stopped at once. Like it or not, the mutiny, this disruptive rebellion will be stopped at once!

B.   This might do it. You will take Joe Guerilla aside for a private conference. You will let him know that you "appreciate" his efforts to help manage the group. (Thus, letting him know that you are "on" to him.) Because he does have a strong influence, however, you will suggest that, together, you and he can really make this "work out right for everyone." On a confidential basis, you will promise him some *special reward* for his cooperation. You know that he really does have the company's best interests at heart, just as you do. You have the authority and capability to provide special rewards or incentives to those who make extraordinary contributions to the growth and success of the group effort. This might make him a willing ally, helping enforce your instructions rather than appearing to contradict them.

C.   You are not, basically, the kind of manager who believes in "letting nature take its course." You believe in giving mother nature a helping hand once in a while in order to achieve an objective. However, this could be an exceptional case. Try cooling it for a while. Joe Guerilla will probably trip himself up, eventually losing the control and influence he seems to have over your group. Sure, you'd like to get this matter over with. However, control your impatience, time is on your side!

D.   How well do you really know this fellow you call Joe Guerilla? Yes, he has worked for and with you for some time. You've made sales calls with him and seen him operate "under fire." You know what "makes him tick." But, you know what makes him tick as a sales man. Do you really know him as an individual? Do you know what his personal needs and motivations are? Is it possible there is more to him than you realize? Of course, one could say this about anybody. But, what about Joe Guerilla? He's been a special, high-achieving sales person. He loves selling. He's told you this often and you've seen how turned on he gets in a tough-sell situation. Since he appears to be part of the present problem, you will take time to get to know him as an individual.

You will begin with some assumptions. He doesn't really want your job. He's not competing with you. That isn't his style and it isn't where he's coming from. Perhaps he is on some sort of "ego trip," satisfying a need for recognition, status, and power by becoming a dominant personality in the sales group. Then again, maybe he didn't really ask for the role of Joe Guerilla, the underground fighter. Possibly, there's a falldown somewhere else that he is trying to compensate for. Assume also that he is well aware of the fact he is treading a dangerous "mill," influencing the group without jeopardizing his job by pushing you too far.

In Option D you will enlist his cooperation by making certain he fully understands the logic and reasoning on which your decisions and your instructions to the group are based. When he understands the "why" of things, he might just become one of your strongest supporters. Much better a "Joe Buddy" than a "Joe Guerilla!"

E.   Another option occurs to you that sounds pretty good, and you are wise to consider it. Have individual discussions with the members of your sales group. This could very well be an appropriate moment for a "friendly confrontation" with each sales person, letting them know that you are perfectly well aware of what is going on. You are a professional sales person yourself. Use those tried-and-true persuasive powers of yours to win them over to your side. Point out the dangers of taking sides with Joe Guerilla. It never hurts, does it, to remind your people who it is that gives them their periodic performance reviews and appraisals and who it is that recommends people for promotions?

After all, participating in an active resistance is the same as *insubordination.* Isn't it the wrong thing to do? This one-on-one approach may take time. You have to get around to each member of the group individually. However, if it works it's a very good use of your time and energies in getting everybody back on the same track—the one you've selected for this "train."

DISCUSSION OF OPTIONS (PRO AND CON)

There are important environmental factors that enable or cause the informal leader to emerge. When the informal leader appears to be directing a rebellion among his peers, the formal leader is wise to search within his group for signs of frustration and needs that are not being satisfied. It is entirely possible that you, as the sales manager, are not paying enough attention to the *emotional* needs of the members of the group. It is also possible that you are too authoritarian, that your people fear you because you are *too strong.* That is to say you come across as the *boss,* always looking at the numbers and rarely at the people. This isn't unusual, especially when the sales manager himself is operating under severe pressure from his own manager. When we are "uptight," our perspectives tend to become confused and we may, without fully realizing it, transfer some of this unpleasantness to our subordinates.

Another possibility is that the dynamic, outgoing, expressive and exciting personality of the person you refer to as Joe Guerilla is exceptionally attractive to his peers. Contrast his personality with your own. Perhaps you are or have become somewhat withdrawn lately, less communicative than you usually are.

The point is quite simply that the emergence of a Joe Guerilla as an informal leader is invariably indicative of a troubled relationship between the formal leader and his subordinates. You may have known Joe Guerilla as a top-notch sales man. His role as a member of the "underground" is new to you and probably just as new to him. You may wonder why he hasn't come right out and told you you were in some sort of jam. But, maybe you have not made such candid talk appear welcome.

You, as the manager, must examine the situation carefully. Has your management style changed recently? Is your style appropriate to the needs and the occasions when you are called upon to express your managerial skills? If you have been coming on too strongly, you might have generated feelings of insecurity. This could cause a grouping under an informal leader whose personality and behavior provide reinforcement of the need for a sense of security and recognition.

Thus, you are identifying causes and effects. You are reestablishing your identity through, if necessary, a modification of your own behavior.

A. This option might appeal to the authoritarian leader (whose authoritarian behavior probably got him into trouble in the first place). This option completely ignores the possible existence of a basic problem in interpersonal relationships between the formal leader and his subordinates. If the manager has been weak, this sudden show of strength will hardly be convincing. Can a weak manager sustain a show of strength? Probably not. The members of the group will recognize this, bide their time, give insincere promises to "obey," and renew their allegiance to the informal leader, Joe Guerilla. If the manager has been authoritarian and dictatorial all the time, Option A could reinforce the need for the role played by Joe Guerilla as the source of emotional security. A confrontation of the kind this option suggests could erupt into an open and angry series of arguments and personality conflicts between the manager and his subordinates. Or, it may be greeted with stony silence; the manager, in effect, talking to himself. No, this particular option is not the way to solve the problem.

B. Why should Joe Guerilla cooperate with you? If he enjoys his role as informal leader why should he give it up? Why should he even admit to being Joe Guerilla? If he enjoys the role, accepting the bribe, the special reward you offer him, will remove him from the position of control that he enjoys. You may succeed in "buying him out," but you will not have succeeded in defining or curing the basic illness, the environment that brought the situation into existence. You may have "disarmed" this Joe Guerilla, but you may have also opened the way for a *new* informal leader to emerge. No, this is not the long-term resolution that you are seeking.

C.   Uless you are a compulsive gambler, you will stay away from this option. The informal leader may "trip himself up," in time, but there could be a replacement ready to pick up the role. This is a *high-risk* option, to say the least. Furthermore, while waiting for nature to run her course, the quota is not being met. Targets are slipping more and more during each day of waiting. Enough said?

D.   Joe Guerilla would probably prefer to gain his recognition and status through his performance in the field as a top sales person. His motivation is to help the members of the group, his peers, to satisfy their needs. He has an ability to understand their needs. He may have some difficulty articulating their needs. His style is primarily intuitive—while untrained as a manager he is exceptionally skilled in interpersonal relationships. With encouragement from you, he could become an unusually valuabie link in the communications chain that has weakened, or even broken, between you and your sales people.

You can, for everyone's well being, draw out Joe Guerilla, help him define with you the faults in the environment or in your own management style that have contributed to the problem. Joe Guerilla can be a positive sounding board, enabling you to hear and comprehend the messages that are being sent to you by the very existence of this situation. As you quickly modify your own behavior, Joe Guerilla will once again turn his full attention to "quota-busting." The informal leader will cease to exist simply because there will be no need for someone to play such a role. The entire group will turn its attention and emotions to sales performance. Their needs will be met by you, the formal leader, and Joe Guerilla will indeed become Joe Buddy! Yes, Option D appears to be the long-term answer. But, what about Option E?

E.   Some theorists of human behavior would support this approach as a workable option. However, if it works, it works only with totally unskilled (probably unschooled) labor—rarely with professional or skilled line or staff people. This is the pure use of *threat* as a means to problem solving; a certain and sure way to create an exodus of your best and most creative people. This is neither a short- nor long-term solution. It was included among the options as a model of one of the *poorest* approaches to manage a conflict.

Back to Option D. Go with it!

4 NO-NO

The Implacable, Constant, and Nonstop Complainer

Every section, group, and department has one of this kind. No matter how hard you try to avoid the experience, you can't escape the *No-No* personality. What's worse, you usually have no way of spotting this type of person in advance. You know he's on board only *after* you've hired him.

NEVER A GOOD WORD

He's the one who is never satisfied and always unhappy with everything that's said or done. You would give almost anything to hear one *positive* word from him—about anything! In some companies, this person is known as a *malcontent*. Usually, problems with malcontents tend to work themselves out rather quickly. Peer pressure has been known to make them to "shape up or ship out!"

But, there is a very important difference here. You don't want No-No to ship out. You want him to shape up because he's a real producer, a top performer as far as selling your company's products and services is concerned. Inside the company he's a big pain. You have to hold yourself in check when you speak with him or include him in brainstorming meetings. Wouldn't you enjoy letting off steam by shouting *you are fired?* What a mixed bag of benefits. He's a high achiever, but his vocabulary seems limited to low-level negative phrases like "No, No."

Your competitors would love to have him working for them. They may not know about his negative personality inside the company. They certainly do know that he is always taking orders away from them; and wouldn't he be great as a member of their sales force? If they only knew the cost!

When anyone suggests he adopt a more positive expression, he says "I am not a robot! I have the right to question things around here! Why am I expected to go along with everyone else? Doesn't my opinion count for something?" It sounds a bit like democratic soap-boxing, and it is very hard to counter his arguments. Obviously, No-No is not aware of the disturbing effect he has on everyone.

What should you do? What can you do? A crisis is at hand that could easily cause a nasty blowup of tempers between No-No and his peers. You want to avoid such unproductive and nasty scenes, but you don't really want to avoid the situation. You want to get to the fundamental cause of this unpleasantness, and resolve it so that you can retain No-No's skills but get rid of his negativism. He is an unusually intelligent person, but perhaps a bit overly emotional in his responses. What should you do?

You have to present several options to your own boss who has become aware of No-No and the effect he is having on the group. You know that there is more than one solution to the problem, but only one is best for the long term.

THESE ARE YOUR OPTIONS

A.   He's a human being, after all. You are seriously considering talking with your sales team and asking them to make a stronger effort to put up with No-No's miserable disposition. Who knows how much he is really hurting deep down inside. His behavior may not change, but you and your people can learn to go along with it by trying to understand No-No a little better.

B.   Ask personnel, or one of No-No's peers who gets along reasonably well with him, to take him aside and make him completely aware of the effect he has on others. Maybe he'll change.

C.   You will apply pressure on No-No. Lean on him. Perhaps he needs a *critical parent;* a "throwback" to his childhood and tough taskmasters who might have dominated his formative years. Sometimes the sales manager has to play the role of "parent" in order to get positive responses from his subordinates. This could be an example.

D.   Then, again, is No-No the one at fault? Or, is it the company? His peers? Could it be you, personally? Search for the right timing and the opportunity to have a "friendly" chat with him. Surely, with your skills in interpersonal relationships, you should have no trouble getting him to "open up" and level with you about what's really bugging him. Play it from there, by ear.

E.   Does he have enough challenge for his high intelligence and energy level? Try *job enrichment.* Assign him tasks that offer greater challenges to him, that let him know you have confidence in his skills and judgment as a professional sales person. This is a form of recognition and ego-support that high achievers need. Don't give him more *work,* give him more *challenge.* Maybe that's where his head is at.

DISCUSSION OF OPTIONS (PRO AND CON)

You really are on the "spot." You are an experienced, professional sales man and sales manager. You are not a trained psychologist, therapist, rabbi, priest, or minister. There are practical limits, also, to just how much time you can dedicate to any one person in your group. Your "bottom line" tasks are heavy, time consuming, and demanding. However, you accomplish your tasks through the skills and productivity of your crew, and No-No is one of the best on this score. You have no choice but to make and take time to resolve this—*without firing him.* Let's examine the probable effects of each of the five options you have identified and are considering.

A.   Some members of your sales team are more productive than others; but, all are top-notch in making quotas. Perhaps it would not be fair to expect or to even ask them to continue to put up with No-No's behavior indefinitely. Are you "playing favorites?" This might stir up some other gripes from the rest of the group. Also, can you really spare extra time to spend with him? Can you estimate *how much extra time?* Move on.

B.   This is a "cop-out" and personnel will recognize it as such. Personnel is there for many reasons. Arbitration, mediation, or intervention in interpersonal conflicts are not among them. This is your job. If you want to transfer or replace No-No, personnel will help you. They will, if they are able to, advise you on how you might deal or cope with the situation. But, you should not try to find a substitute who will do your job. This option could backfire. Next, please.

C.   You could be right about his need for a parent substitute as a cause of his negative behavior. This doesn't mean he would accept you in the role of parent. He might resent such an action on your part and build defenses against you. Another possible, but undesirable, response is that he might appear to comply, as some children do. But, the basically negative behavior might merely go "underground" for a while and, with a fierce release of internal pressures, explode suddenly into a fierce personality conflict and blowup that could make matters worse than before. Move on, again.

D.   If No-No is wrong, how are you, untrained as a psychologist or spiritual leader, going to successfully show him the "error of his ways" and bring about positive modification of his behavior? Suppose the company is at fault? Are you able to change the company to suit him? Yes, a sales manager should have skills in behavior modification. However, this is one of the most difficult things for anyone to try to do without special training. You might get him to "open up" with you. Are you sure he won't be "giving you a line?" Is he able to accurately define his own problem for you? This is hazardous to your own position. The situation could escalate, getting worse rather than better. This looks very much like a "no-no" approach, a "no-win" resolution.

E.   People such as No-No usually have a low self-esteem. They need recognition to help them build confidence in themselves. They do *not* need special favors. Their keen awareness of their environments enables them to instantly recognize sincerity as easily as they do artificially. Such people usually respond favorably to *job enrichment* (challenge), but not to *job enlargement* (more work).

For example, determine which types of accounts he is most effective with. You will probably find they are the *tough* ones, those that others in the group are afraid of or can't handle too well. Assign these accounts to him. Tell him why you are doing so. This is *recognition!*

Few people who find satisfaction and personal reward in their work behave as No-No does. With the support of your own supervisor, this becomes the most logical of the options. It prevents escalation of the problem, builds order-writing levels, and can eliminate the personality conflicts. If it works, everybody wins. You can anticipate that No-No will respond to the recognition you have offered by suggesting some alternative courses of action—positive ones that will have a good chance of winning in the long run because No-No will, quite likely and without prodding, develop a strong *personal commit-ment to making them work.*

What is the probability for long-term success? Option E offers you and everyone involved a *no-lose* pathway to resolving the conflict.

5 WHAT-DID-HE-SAY

Can You Bridge This Communications Gap?

"I've taken many ace sales men and made lousy district managers out of them!" Unfortunately, too many sales managers, good ones, are able to make this statement. Each time it happens, the lesson is relearned that there are real differences between being a *quota-buster* and a *good manager*. "I've got a half-a-dozen sales people on my team who can outsell me anytime!" This is the realistic sales manager who isn't embarrassed, ashamed, or too proud to admit there are others who can and do outproduce him in order-writing. But, he is the first to recognize and describe the significant differences between *selling* and *managing* those who do the selling.

Well, knowledgeable, experienced, and astute as you are, you may have "blown" it this time. One of your district sales managers, recently promoted by you from field sales man because he was so "hot" with customers, seems to be having more trouble in his district. Orders have fallen off; more than just a bit, too. Enough of a falloff so that the home office is wondering what's going on. And, you don't have the answer. But, you know you had better develop a plan of action.

Of course, before you can find a solution you have to define the problem. You tell the district manager you are coming to his "territory" to review the sales plan and the quota.

The interesting thing is that both he and you had put a lot of time and thought into the plan and quota, had arrived at a general consensus, and felt confident about the future. His enthusiasm and commitment seemed very real. You have no reason to believe they were anything but sincere. But, your own supervisor has asked you for an interim report—a reaffirmation of the forecasts and budgets you had presented at the start of the fiscal period. At this moment, you are not as confident as you were about the new district manager and his territory's performance.

A SEA OF CONFUSION

It doesn't take a pro, such as you are, too long to discover— during your visit to the troubled district and in your talks with the sales group—that not too many of the people in the group really understand the plan, quota, which direction to go in, or which accounts to concentrate on.

It had all seemed so clear when you discussed the details of the plan with your district manager. Why isn't it clear to his sales people? In fact, why do they appear so confused? They are all experienced in sales. Nevertheless, things are *not at all clear* to them. This has all the earmarks of a *communication problem!* All of your doubts are eliminated when you hear the nickname the whole office has given to the district manager—*What-Did-He-Say.*

You ask, as is your prerogative, to see the manager's "letterbook" (his file copies of internal correspondence and memos for the past three months). Sure enough, there it is! Either the guy can't communicate clearly or is deliberately causing confusion through misinformation or distortion. You wonder if he is ignoring your mutual agreements, or is he just a lousy communicator—*what did he say?*

You have to learn the facts!

A candid discussion with *What-Did-He-Say* is an essential part of getting directly to the root of the problem. You let him know what you perceive and you expect him to recognize that you are trying to help him do a good job. You have no reason to believe or even think he is deliberately working against you or the company. He is quite open with you on every single matter. In fact, he is sincerely pleased that you came. He knows he needs help, and he respects your managerial skills.

He admits he senses that his people don't always follow his instructions. Sometimes, they even seem to ignore or go against them. His files show how hard he has tried to communicate. The results, unhappily, show failure. He is honest. You do find the cause of the problem.

But, how do you define the problem to him and develop a workable solution? It is obvious to you that every one of his memos is filled with ambiguities, contradictions, and confusing statements. You recognize that he is giving *accurate* instructions *inaccurately!* A genuine, gold-plated *communications problem!* It is easy to see now why everyone is so confused, and very easy to understand the nickname *What-Did He Say.*

Now you have to define the problem and develop a solution as part of your status report to your own supervisor. Obviously, you are going to have to revise your near-term orders forecast, at least temporarily. You are not ready to change your forecast for the year. However, it would not be realistic to expect to make quota in this specific district, in this fiscal period, and under the present set of circumstances.

You can't hide the problem. Nor do you want to hide it from your own supervisor. This isn't your style. However, when you do describe the problem to him you know you will be expected to review the options that are open to you. Again, the very *last* thing you want to do is fire the guy. He is a very productive sales man. Your competitors know this as well as you do. He could probably walk out of your company and right into a key job with any one of your competitors. They don't know the things you have just learned about his weakness in communicating with others. But, you don't want to give them a chance to find out. There is a better way, you know. More than one, in fact.

THESE ARE YOUR OPTIONS

A.   You know the problem. But, it is just as important for What-Did-He Say to recognize his own shortcomings and see for himself how he has been confusing his sales people. With firm yet gentle handling, you will help him make the "discovery." Then, together, you will develop a plan of action that will change his name to "Mr. Clear!" One way to accomplish this could be to send him, at company expense, to seminars on *"oral communications"* and on *"writing-to-be-understood."* Training of this type is sponsored by many private and public organizations, since the problem isn't unusual.

B.   How about putting together your own in-house seminar/workshop on *communication skills?* You are considered an outstanding communicator—always getting your point across clearly and concisely. Why not conduct the program yourself? Make it a company-wide program, written and directed by yourself. Then, lots of people would benefit from your skills.

C.   On the other hand, seminars and workshops take too much time away from field-sales work. Consider the value of ordering some of the best books on the subject of *written communication.* The budget has a "training" account that can pick up the tab as tax-deductible educational expense for the company. Give the books to What-Did-He-Say. In fact, maybe you can avoid the need for a candid discussion that might be personally embarrasssing to both of you by giving him the books. You're pretty sure he'll get the message.

There's knowledge to be gained entirely from the exercise of reading.

D.   Haven't you been writing letters, reports, plans, and memoranda for years? Why not write a *manual on communications* yourself? Distribute the manual to everyone in your sales group with special directions to What-Did-He-Say to be sure to read the instructions and put them into practice. Make it part of the job responsibility for all your managers and supervisors to read and understand the "how-to" sections.

E.   How about this one? Time is short. Take on the communications chores yourself. When you issue a directive or a memo, distribute it to everyone who is affected by it. Perhaps this may tend to "bypass" formal channels of communication but it will get your message across without confusion, and without comments such as "What did he say."

F.   Some things you have to learn to accept as they are. What-Did-He-Say types are a burden that successful sales managers have to live with. There's a very strong possibility that anything you do to try to correct the situation will fail. Murphy's Law says anything that can go wrong, will; Riley's Law says that all efforts to correct it will fail! Why fuss—he's a top sales man and that's a skill that's hard to find!

DISCUSSION OF OPTIONS (PRO AND CON)

A discussion of the positive and negative aspects of each of the options will help remove, or at least diminish, the confusion and frustration you may be feeling right now.

A.   The most effective way to approach this is to enable What-Did-He-Say to discover his own shortcomings as a communicator. Usually, people who do become aware of their faults and the effects they have on their peers try to develop solutions of their own to which they become strongly committed. A commitment dramatically improves the probabilities for success. You can expect the morale and attitude of your district manager to improve more rapidly, thereby creating an environment that will inspire and motivate his subordinates to new levels of success in their sales responsibilities. You will work *with* him. *Everybody wins!* But, let's not stop here; let's examine the remaining options.

B.   In-house or outside-the-house seminars and workshops should be left to those who specialize in this type of activity. You may be a good communicator, but you have no credentials as an instructor (beyond the usual and very valuable one-on-one sidewalk critiques after a sales call has been made). You may gain a "warm feeling" from giving a seminar to your crew, but the desired result will probably not be attained this way. If you want to add seminars and workshops to your training program, fine, *but call in an expert.*

C.   This is as subtle as a rock falling on a big toe! Your intentions are good, but your message is as vague and unclear as those sent by the guy you are trying to help. Can't you hear your district manager asking, after the books arrive, "what did he say?" Books contain knowledge, yes. However, What-Did-He-Say needs the benefit of your experience as well. Give the books to him, and to anyone else you think might benefit from them—but only as part of or in addition to Option A.

D.   You certainly are multi-talented—a writer as well as a teacher, sales man, and sales manager! Do you really have time to research, write, publish, and distribute a technical manual on communications. Your boss will probably suggest your time would be better spent in more directly productive areas—such as going back to field sales! If you are serious about assembling a training manual of your own, budget for it and hire a professional with related experience—the same thing you prescribe for yourself when hiring a sales person. You wouldn't necessarily hire a writer for an important sales job. Option D is not likely to get the desired result. It's bad for the image, too.

E.   Where have you heard this one before: "If you want

to get the job done right, you have to do it yourself"? The shortest distance between two points is a straight line—except in a formal organization. Bypassing your own staff, your own "chain of communications," can ultimately have everybody in your group, section, department, or division reporting *directly to you!* If you believe that the only way to get the job done right is to do it yourself, you have a problem of your own—you are unable to delegate authority and responsibility. This can put a *low ceiling* on your own advancement within your company. The only way to grow is to build an organization of competent professionals who, as they rise, will lift you to higher levels.

F.   Accept the situation as it is? You are right to consider this option. But, the situation is *unacceptable* to say the least. Murphy and Riley and their entertaining "laws" are just that—entertaining, but not useful here in building your staff, your department, and your own career.

There is only *one* option for you—A.

6 ONLY-WAY

He has the Only Answer to Every Question

This member of your sales team always has *the* answer, always tells the others *what* to do and *how* to do it! When choosing a course of action, he knows he's right—and everyone else is wrong. His way is the *only* way. Every other idea presented by anyone else is a bad idea. *Only-Way* seems to wear earmuffs; he never really hears what others are suggesting. Even without asking any questions, he has what he's sure is the right answer. His way is the *only way* to go!

Only-Way has a very outstanding sales record. He's a fine sales man. His behavior with customers is excellent. But, with his peers, or even with you, he is best described as "often offensive." Even when his ideas are good ones—and he always has many ideas which often turn out to be the best of all other suggestions—it's the way he presents them that gets everybody's back up.

He is opinionated, argumentative, and downright unpleasant in the way he goes about telling the group how right he is and how wrong the rest of them are. Only-Way has a strong and even overwhelming personality, but it is hardly a likeable one.

Only-Way has assumed the privilege of "steam-rollering" right over his peers and their ideas. He has even done it to you. He lacks all flexibility or receptivity to the idea of compromise or consensus. Your group has spent untold time and energy trying to get him to consider other options and approaches to problems and other answers to questions.

The resentment toward Only-Way is interfering with the growth of the sales force as a team. Now, for everyone's sake, you must step in and steer this difficult sales person toward a more receptive attitude; that is, toward a way of behavior that will give "equal time" to his peers and a demonstration of respect for their viewpoints.

THESE ARE YOUR OPTIONS

A.   You might decide this is the time for you to manage as a forceful leader—to be a dictator! It may be appropriate now, even though it may not be your usual style, for you to order Only-Way to change the way he behaves toward his peers. And, while you are at it, you might just let him know he does the same thing to you and you don't admire him for it. It is your responsibility to nurture team spirit and cooperation and, as manager of the group, you must insist that Only-Way become a more cooperative member of the group. After all, he is having a very bad effect on team spirit. He is fighting all your best efforts to build morale, positive attitudes, and a motivated *esprit de corps.* It is patently illogical to assume that any *one* person could have the *only* correct answer every single time! You will, in plain language, order him to discontinue his rude and opinionated behavior.

B.   Line up the other members of the sales team as your allies in a "battle" against Only-Way. You will talk to each of them, telling them you are very well aware of how irritating and disturbing Only-Way is. Ask each of them to report to you every instance of Only-Way's rude, undemocratic, and inflexible behavior. Then, you will have plenty of "ammunition" for a confrontation with Only-Way. This ties in with the "orders" you will give him in Option A.

C.   Take him to your leader! Let him hear all about his unwelcome behavior directly from the top. This will make him aware of the fact that his poor personal conduct is well known, that his behavior is unacceptable, and that he'd better change. The implicit threat to his job, coming from his boss's boss, might underscore your own arguments, might make him broaden his outlook and recognize that others might actually be as right as he thinks he always is.

D.   You could assume that Only-Way doesn't really have any awareness of the effect he has on other people—that is, the sometimes overbearing and irritating way he comes across. Without anger or threats, you will tell him that you perceive the elements of a conflict, a problem in personal relationships that must be solved. Continuing, you will let him know that you—and the entire sales group—value his contributions to overall performance and productivity. But, the interpersonal situation needs to be improved dramatically so that the group can continue to grow as a *team*. Together, you and he will work to resolve the conflict so that nobody loses and nobody is embarrassed. You can help him understand that, during all problem-solving discussions, each person must listen to the viewpoints of others and respect their rights to open expression. Tell him quite directly that he can enhance his effectiveness by doing just that. You will propose a personal contract between yourself and Only-Way: In the future, you will let him know privately when you and others feel he is coming across too irritatingly, much too strongly.

DISCUSSION OF OPTIONS (PRO AND CON)

What makes Only-Way so overbearing? The cause can probably be traced to the influence or example of a controlling parent or relative, a tough-minded school teacher, a hard-nosed supervisor, or other similar role model from his formative years. This could mean that Only-Way is receptive to guidance. Very likely, he could use a boost to his self-esteem and self-discipline and benefit from advice and counsel in improving his interactions with other people. Perhaps he is "hurting" deep down inside and his unpleasantness is in reality an attempt, although not a terribly effective one, to protect his ego. These are the probable effects of the options that were offered.

A.   Assume that Only-Way's behavior developed because of too much exposure to dictatorial leaders in the past and too little exposure to people who know how to solve problems so that everybody wins and nobody loses. Assume he is interested in the development of the team, but just doesn't know how to demonstrate that interest. He is not likely to heed direct orders that are issued to him. This would be too reminiscent of those disciplinarians who unknowingly overused and sometimes abused the authority they held over him. He may, at first, follow a command but, in the long run, his defense mechanisms may well discount your orders as if he had never heard them. This option may result in a very *short-term* improvement, but holds no hope for the long-term success you want to achieve. You had better take a look at another option.

B.   This one postpones the eventual confrontation indicated in Option A. It also makes you seem petty, perhaps a bit underhanded, weak, and ineffective as a leader. It is not likely that others in the group would "tattle" on a peer, even though, as with Only-Way, his behavior makes them quite uncomfortable. In addition, this course of action exposes you to reports that are likely to be inaccurate, distorted by personal feelings of animosity, or resulting from some other "axe to grind."

C.   This exposure of Only-Way to official examination and the implicit threat to his job security can only lower his self-esteem and could intensify his undesirable behavior. Also, marching him into your boss's office allows two inferences, both reflecting on your capabilities: (1) you can't solve your problems without direct hand-holding from above, and (2) you have created a confrontation that makes Only-Way appear "guilty until proven innocent." What's more, it could make him begin a serious search for another job—which is not at all what you are aiming for. This is even less desirable than the two previous options. Reject this one!

D.   You're probably right that Only-Way doesn't have a clue as to why he gets along so poorly with his fellow sales people. He does believe in his ideas, but he may also be unaware that the way he expresses them is too often rude, interruptive, and overbearing. He probably doesn't have the slightest idea why his peers react so negatively to him. It is very likely that he has many questions about himself that are desperately in need of answers. He may very well have some fundamental difficulties in framing the questions that he has about himself. Certainly, he needs help in this area so that meaningful and actionable answers can be developed.

Choose an appropriate time for a private conversation, when tempers are cool and reason prevails. Describe to him how you see his behavior and the problems it seems to create. Tell him you believe it can be improved. Help him recognize the problem. Help him confront it without hostility or anxiety. Listen carefully and reactively to everything he says. Maintain a friendly problem-solving let's-do-it-together ambience.

This is the first stage in solving the problem so that the morale, attitude, and productivity of the entire team can be improved—contributing to the company's profitability and, just as important, to everyone's satisfaction in doing the job well, and in attaining the group's objectives.

You will propose to Only-Way that, because others in the group are involved in the situation, a problem-solving group session should be arranged. At this meeting all persons will be invited to make constructive suggestions on how the environment can be improved. No, this is not to be a session in which Only-Way is to become a target for anyone to shoot at. It always takes at least two people to have a conflict and the rest of the group must share the responsibility, along with you, for the current state of affairs. There will be no finger-pointing or name-calling permitted, either directly or by innuendo. Everyone knows there is a conflict, so it is pointless to belabor the fact. It is more meaningful to ask the question "where do we go from here" and for everyone to offer helpful answers.

You will propose an orderly and structured process of conflict resolution in which there are no losers. Together, Only-Way and the other members of the sales force, guided (not directed) by you, will define the disagreement from every point of view. Next, the group will list and discuss each avenue or approach that might solve the apparent problem. Through careful appraisal and discussion of the advantages of each of the possible approaches, the group will reach a consensus. Through this method, a specific direction will be developed for Only-Way and for each member of the team to move toward—*together*. Everyone who has participated in the decision-making process will feel personally committed to making it work.

Now, as manager or supervisor of the group, you will guide the formulation of a series of specific steps to assure success in resolving the problem—to which, you will make it clear, everyone has made a contribution. Then you will help establish a timetable acceptable to all. At specified critical points along the way, the group will meet to evaluate its own progress. Our friend Only-Way will have an equal role and voice in these periodic evaluations. Any stumbling blocks or back-sliding will be discussed in a constructive environment—not with Only-Way being placed under a magnifying lens—with every member of the group having an equal opportunity for self-expression and for making a contribution to the solution. This is "teamwork!"

The prospect is good with Option D that Only-Way will develop a more satisfying relationship with each of his peers and, of course, with you. The group wins. The company wins. There are no losers. Only-Way may, very soon, acquire a new nickname, "Our-Way." Option D is best—and it represents the management style with which you want your name, fame, and fortune as a manager to be most closely identified.

7 DASHER

He Works in Unpredictable
Fits and Starts

Articulate! Bright! Sociable! Likeable! He works like a tiger—
sometimes. At other times he barely works at all. This is the
problem. He turns his energies on and off as if they were
water from a tap. They flow when he's "thirsty" and, even
then, they don't flow with any sort of predictability. He
works at his own pace, appearing to ignore the "speed" of
the group and the needs and deadlines of the company.
Slowly, slowly he moves. Then, in a surprise burst of activity, he *dashes ahead!*

ALWAYS IN THE WRONG GEAR

Unfortunately, *Dasher* is invariably out of step with the rest
of the team. He's certainly a top producer; no doubt about
this. However, you realize you can't depend on him for consistently top results in sales. You know he is capable of very
fine things; but, his start/stop approach to work keeps you
sitting on the edge of your seat. This is especially evident

toward the end of the month when you have to file your report on actual bookings versus budget, when the pressure is on you to provide updates for your forecasts.

There's more to this than your own needs. The frustration is shared by the group that wants to become a highly effective team. Dasher often performs brilliantly, works hard, and can display great creativity as a sales person. Too often, however, Dasher goes into one of his "hardly working" phases when his contribution is most sorely needed.

You are not a psychologist, but you do have lots of experience dealing with people in the real world of sales. You've learned from practical experience that Dasher is afraid of failure. You are willing to bet that his self-esteem is actually as low as his fear of failure is high. He's reluctant to reach for high goals. His expectations are low. This generally leaves him working at levels that are well below his potential and his capability. He may see risk as a pathway to failure rather than to success. So, he plays it "safe." Once in a while, relatively speaking, he loses his fears and charges forward; the *Dasher* in him takes control and he gains some confidence. But, he is unable to sustain this positive effort. Negativism sets in again, fear takes over, and he returns to his intolerably slow pace.

If he weren't such a top producer, and if the averaging effect of his on-again/off-again performance were not so great, you'd transfer him and restore some stability to your work as sales manager. But, there has to be another way to sort this out, a way that will create a balance between your needs and his methods.

Others in your sales group are showing signs of uncontrollable displeasure with Dasher and his work habits. Others outside the group notice and comment about Dasher—*will he make it?* This also implies doubt that *you* will make it to the end of the sales period. You know your own boss is aware of the problem. The sudden "ups" and "downs" are quite visible in the weekly sales summaries. The suspenseful buildup to the end of the fiscal period is not an activity in which he cares to participate. The situation just isn't correcting itself. It might even get worse if you don't step in to make it better. The pointer is aiming in your direction.

The wise thing to do is examine your options and discuss them with your boss. Of course, you will make a strong, logical recommendation for the option that offers the best promise for long-term results.

THESE ARE YOUR OPTIONS

A. Your choice of action might be to apply gentle pressure whenever Dasher slows down—just enough pressure to break up his pattern and get him back into phase with the group and the task. You would leave him alone when he's doing well (always a good idea, you believe) and pressure him when he starts to slow down. This could tend to even out the peaks and valleys of his work pace.

B. What our friend Dasher needs is a strong "dose" of old-fashioned *discipline*. This will make him change his work habits. And, you know exactly how to do the discipline bit. Tell him, right up front, what your perceptions are about his work habits. Tell him about the effect they have on the team and its productivity. Tell him exactly how the other team players feel about his last-minute dashes to make quota— which he usually exceeds—thus proving that he is generally working below his full level of capability. As a matter of fact, you can point to other members of the team as examples of the kind of consistency you expect from him. You are proud of the professionalism of your sales group. Point out to him that they can serve as good role models for him to emulate. Make your expectations clear to him. Set up unambiguous rules and standards of performance. You will let him know that you and he will get together every so often to review progress.

C. You might decide that you can help prop up his performance; but first you have to discover why it is so uneven. Maybe something in his personal life is bothering or distracting him from his work. Salving this "itch" might smooth out his performance, making Dasher more consistent and predictable. Let him know that he can depend on your knowledge and experience and rely on you for support. He can lean on you for strength, counsel, and guidance. Every good manager provides moral support for his subordinates—right? You want to be his friend.

D.   The first stop in problem-solving is awareness. People with problems can't do anything about solving them until they become fully aware of and accept the fact that they have problems. So, it's up to you to help Dasher see the full effect of his erratic pace. It hurts him, his peers, the company, and doesn't help you do your job. Without any threats, implied or explicit, you will discuss the situation with him, calmly and as impersonally as possible. (Not too easy, given the seriousness of the matter.) There are some good things going for both of you. He is intelligent, bright, and the acceptance of his peers is important to him. Of course, he is the only one who can actually change any undesirable work habits. You can be the catalyst for change by helping him understand what he is doing—or not doing—showing him how he can improve his overall performance and become a welcome member of the sales team.

DISCUSSION OF OPTIONS (PRO AND CON)

Make sure your assessment of Dasher's potential and performance level is realistic. Review what you know about his capabilities based on his actual sales track record. Is it possible that his previous outstanding performance was due to luck rather than talent and work? Is he truly an underachiever, capable of sustained work activity and continuously excellent performance? He is a highly intelligent individual who understands the nature of his work and the team's objectives. You have every reason to believe that he can work at a more consistent pace and at a higher level of productivity. Perhaps you have not communicated your expectations clearly enough and, therefore, Dasher may not have an adequate understanding of what is expected of him beyond the aggregate, statistical aspect of his job. Perhaps he feels and thinks much like the school child who appears to pay little attention to the daily requirements of the teacher and curriculum, but amazes everyone with his excellent performance on examination day.

One of the things a *good* manager does is help build high levels of self-expectation in each of the people who work with him. You accept this as your personal responsibility.

Think about this apparent anomaly for a bit. Sometimes individuals with high intelligence levels require *more* explanation than others. He may actually be thinking on a "fast track" and looking far ahead into the future, more so than most people do. He may be visualizing situations, challenges, and obstacles that haven't yet occurred to any of the others, possibly not even to you. Dasher may be reluctant to talk out loud about some of the things that he perceives. This awareness of the future may combine with an adequate supply of information to inhibit his day-to-day enthusiasm and performance. Make sure you have explained your expectations and the company's expectations in precise detail to every member of the sales team.

This is the professional way. This is good management. Take time or make time to provide an ample opportunity for questions. And, be aware that there is no such thing as a "stupid" question.

A.   Anyone with rank and authority can apply pressure. That's especially easy for the one with a manager's title. And pressure should work, shouldn't it? You are the boss! But, is this likely to cause any real improvement over the long term, make anyone's performance more consistent with your needs? Or, will it be turning the tap on (when you apply pressure) and turning the tap off (when the pressure is removed)? If you are willing to keep the pressure on all the time, Dasher may well perform at a consistently high level. But, can you or should you do this? You have to think about other people, many other tasks, and your other management responsibilities. Besides, Dasher and his behavior are part of a complex system; the problem needs a more realistic approach. No, this is not the long-term solution you desire.

B.   This has a similarity to Option A, with a strong dose of discipline added. Maybe what Dasher needs is a supervisor who can act as a stern critic. Quite likely, this will bring about an undesirable open confrontation—a blowup from which the only lesson that might be learned is that you have misinterpreted Dasher's needs. If he is an insecure person, any behavior on your part resembling that of a demanding parent could reinforce his feelings of insecurity. What has been an uneven performance might degenerate into nonperformance. Furthermore, the strong discipline might arouse antagonism and resentment which could spill over and affect the entire group's performance. It is not very likely that Dasher has any need for a disciplining critic. Next, please.

C.   Does Dasher want to be "propped up?" Does he feel the need to lean on you for support? This is not very likely, but assume he does feel such a need. Will you be able to provide the right kind of support in an adequate quantity? If he does reveal his innermost thoughts to you, the situation could be beyond your technical skills. What do you do then? You could find yourself in the position of offering support—an offer that is accepted, but which you are not properly equipped to deliver.

Going one step further, assume he accepts your offer of support and you are able to deliver. Wll he be able to accept it with good grace? Or, will he resent you and his dependence on you? Just as children often resent parents on whom they must depend for safety, security, and sustenance, adults in the work group can resent a supervisor on whom they become emotionally and physically dependent. Do you want to continually play the game with Dasher (or with any of your people) of finding the problem, providing the support, engendering resentment, overcoming dependence, facing another problem, and so on? Situations such as these are like closed loops. Once formed, they have no ending. This is more like a "lose-lose" situation; that is, a potential trap. Move on to the next option.

D. Use a one-on-one approach. You and Dasher in an adult relationship will come to a complete recognition and awareness of *Dasher's* start/stop work habit and his last-minute dashes to reach sales goals. Then you can use "active listening" techniques that will encourage him to communicate—to accurately articulate his feelings about his work and his relationship with you. Listening attentively, responsively, and maturely, you will probably learn things you never knew about Dasher's motivations and inner feelings. You will learn how he feels about himself and his expectations from his work.

Maybe he isn't motivated by financial reward. Money won't make him modify his behavior. Maybe his need is for recognition as an achieving individual. Maybe this has been missing or lacking in his day-to-day activities. Is there a possibility that you have been "turning him off" (or not "turning him on") because your own behavior is not truly consistent? Is your praise sincere when given? Do you remember to give praise for work that is well done? Are you abrasive at times? Does your sense of humor have a "bite" to it? It is so easy to hurt feelings with a chance remark that, if carefully thought over, would never have been made or allowed to be misinterpreted? Are you part of Dasher's problem? You can be part of the solution. Listen closely, with an open mind to what Dasher has to say.

You may not be able to solve the personal-life problems he might want to talk about. And, if this is so, you will, with compassion, explain your own limitations in this respect. You can help him see that such problems are being allowed to interfere with his job performance. Review the data relevant to his individual sales record; that is, sales versus time intervals. He will see for himself, if it is the case that his "dips" relate to outside disturbances. This revelation will help him exercise a stronger self-discipline and help him to separate his personal and professional lives.

Perhaps he has become overly dedicated to an outside interest—a side-line business, sport, or hobby. He may not have been quite aware of the effect this had on his work. But, pursue this a bit further. Why does he find it necessary to become so deeply involved with outside activities? It is possible that the work environment (over which you do have some control) does not provide adequate satisfaction for his needs for recognition, belonging, identity, and fulfillment? His tasks at work may not be adequately demanding for a person of his intelligence and talents. He finds he is only able to make quota (or beat it) by working in short bursts of energy—*dashing!*

He has never let you down. But you're afraid that someday he will. You and he must work to prevent this from ever happening. You and he will create an informal "contract." Now that each of you has become aware of the real needs of the other, you will develop a plan (this is the contract) for long-term success. Together, you will create milestones and review-intervals for monitoring progress—your progress as well as his.

Dasher will now recognize your expectations and set new levels of self-expectations. Now that he understands the root causes, and that he can take control of his performance, his work curve should begin to smooth out and reach a consistently high level. He will find new satisfaction from his day-to-day work. He will comprehend the need for consistency in his productivity. And you will have a better understanding of the fact that a *good* manager is responsible for *helping* his people satisfy their needs—as well as the company's needs—whether they be physical, financial, egoistic, or social.

Obviously, Option D is the one you will want to put into practice. You will, without a doubt, have the full support of your own supervisor and the company.

8 BURNING-DECK

Procrastination
Turns to Panic

He was one of the best "players" on the sales team, but that was before you promoted him to district sales manager. You thought he had everything it took to be a manager and respected leader of a sales district. There was no doubt at all in your mind that he was intelligent, articulate, productive, and analytical. You were sure, when you promoted him, that he would know what needed to be done and how to do it compentently. In fact, you really anticipated brilliant creativity and strong strategies.

So, based on the good feelings you had about his capabilities you promoted him, making him sales manager for a district with 12 sales people reporting directly to him. What a grand opportunity for him to learn leadership while continuing to be a producer! Your expectations were high, to say the least.

STORM CLOUDS GATHERING

However, you see several worrisome signs and warnings of what might be the beginnings of serious problems in the district. Sales figures are falling off too rapidly in a district that is not having significant business or economic problems. Your protégé, who had shown such promise, seems to have panicked on several occasions. On the surface, there is no other way to describe some of the unwise and hasty decisions he has been making than to say "he panics." At any rate, that's the way it is being fed back to you from the grapevine. He panics! In fact, you hear he has picked up a nickname since he became the district sales manager—*Burning-Deck*. This has something to do with an old poem or novel about "the boy stood upon the burning deck . . ."

You now admit to yourself that each time you visited the district you sensed, but ignored, the feeling that the ambience had changed. Attitudes had moved from high-key enthusiasm and cheerfulness to low-key activity. The sales people you once knew to be go-getters had a quiet, withdrawn manner bordering on apathy. Absenteeism which, according to your personnel people, is sometimes an indicator of dissatisfaction, had gone up alarmingly. Overall productivity has fallen off and threatens to affect your department's ability to make quota. To add to your sense of doom, several of the district's sales people have asked for transfers or leaves of absence. One of them has quit, and good sales people are very hard to find under the best of circumstances. Now, your man, Burning-Deck, has told you he has to fire one of the sales people. Why? Insubordination, of all things. This is a first for your department!

Obviously, all's not right with this district and you'd better take a very close look. The funny thing is that you find yourself referring to your protégé as Burning-Deck. However, you know that's no way for a senior manager to behave! Recall and face up to your own observations—the things you noted on visits to the district but ignored, hoping they would go away.

The relationships between Burning-Deck and his people were strained. You thought Burning-Deck himself was a bit negative and jumpy. Your questions seemed to irritate him. If you had not pulled back on the pressure, you sensed that tempers might flare, temperatures rise, and things you didn't want to hear or say might have been shouted out loud. You wouldn't face the reality then. Well, you'd better get involved and to the bottom (or on top) of the situation—now! Your own "deck" might start "burning."

It doesn't take long for the awful reality of the situation to become clearer to you. When it comes to making decisions, Burning-Deck is a vacillator. He procrastinates, delays dealing directly with problems, and puts off evaluating an opportunity or a risk until it is too late to call for help or guidance which might reduce the risk and increase the opportunity. He goes into a panic that borders on shock, and that has been having a very bad effect on every one of his subordinates. They need timely decisions and forthright support from their manager. Instead, they get indecision and blame for anything that doesn't work out quite right.

Be careful! You don't want to jump to or arrive at any incorrect conclusions. You must become much more observant and objective now—search for facts, collect data, and apply logic, so to speak. You see almost no participation from Burning-Deck's people during sales meetings. This is not at all like the group of "fire eaters" you used to see. There is no open discussion, creative activity, or much problem-solving or brainstorming for ideas from the "top of the head" that get people turned on. Burning-Deck shows stress and does not seem to be in control. There's no two-way communication. He does all the talking (and you're not sure anyone is listening) during group sessions that are supposed to bring out everyone's participation and best ideas. His people seem almost afraid to tell Burning-Deck anything he might not want to hear.

You wonder if this manager is "inhibiting" the initiative of his people—knocking down their aspirations and diminishing their self-expectations. Is he threatened by his own team's professional competence? And, does it really matter whether or not his actions are deliberate? The effect, regardless of the basic cause, is disastrous. Then again, as the manager who is senior to this district manager, you must define the cause. As with virtually all such situations, unfortunately for many managers, the effect may be obvious but the true cause quite elusive.

Wait, there are more symptoms of trouble that you begin to recognize. (Too bad they weren't so obvious to you some time ago, but they are obvious now.) When he was a sales man, his reports were unusual models of clarity—not cryptic and without any "sales man's shorthand." They were always filled with "meat" and were informative and useful. (You remind yourself of this because you know how sales people hate to write reports. They don't mind verbal reports, but some will do almost anything to avoid writing.) This guy was very different in this respect.

But, now that he is a manager, Burning-Deck's reports take on an aura of emotionalism, finger-pointing, passing blame, and are bogged down in nonconstructive detail. Unlike his old sales-call reports, the new reports rarely provide analyses of risks and opportunities and seldom give facts, data, and figures—the kind of stuff sales planning calls for. You know he has the skills and the knowledge. What happened to them and to him? Did he lose them? How can anyone lose or ever forget these skills?

Time's up! You have to get to the bottom of this, get him back on the track, and get this district's sales activity back up to where it is supposed to be. The pressure on you from your own manager is strong. He wants to know: (1) why is the district doing so poorly, and (2) what are you planning to do about it? If it's a people-problem you'd better handle it, but let him have the real story—effect, cause, and solution. You have several options to review with him, none of which includes firing the man you recently promoted. You've scheduled a meeting with your own manager for a review of the past and a preview of the future.

THESE ARE YOUR OPTIONS

A. You intend to have a private talk with Burning-Deck during which you will level with him, telling him exactly what you see the problem is at the bottom line—falling sales performance. He must take responsibility for his group reaching or beating its quota for sales. You can't manage his group for him; you have other districts for which you are equally responsible. You put him in charge of his sales district, so he'd better "take charge!" He has a time limit to straighten up and do his thing, or you will have to take more drastic action.

B. Your approach will be to get Burning-Deck to admit to himself, and to you, that he is the root of this problem of falling sales and restless troops. You will probe the tender and sore spots, if you have to, in order to make him face up to the reality that he has been blaming others for his own inadequate decision-making practices. It will be made quite clear to him that, from now on, his decisions must be supported by analysis and logic and be free of emotionalism. And, he must be able to describe to you what specific steps he intends to take about improving his group's morale, which may be one of the factors in the alarming drop in productivity.

C. Call in the personnel department or an outside consultant in such matters. Ask for an attitudinal study of Burning-Deck's group. You will insist on anonymity for the individual members of the group so they won't hold back in their responses. This could provide specifics about the situation; that is, viewpoints on sales and the actual impact of Burning-Deck on the group. The employee relations department can also talk with him privately, in a sort of psychologist/counselor role, to determine if he has some outside personal problems that are affecting his behavior. You don't believe you should get involved in this sort of thing directly, because, after all, you are his boss and there is always some measure of threat implied when you get involved with a subordinate's personal situation. Perhaps the employee relations department will want to call in an outside consultant to do the interviewing. This is okay with you, but time is of the essence. Emotionalism has been running the district for too long. Valuable ground has been lost and must be regained fast! This could be the way to regain it.

D.   You recognize that, up to this time, you have been working on assumptions, the grapevine's feedback, and virtually no facts. You accept that you are part of the problem because you ignored the early trouble-signs. Starting with a private conversation with Burning-Deck, you will focus on the visible problem of sales performance as an "effect" of something else. With the district sales manager's help (there, you've stopped using his put-down nickname) you will try to determine the cause or causes of the problem. You will be your usual calm, unruffled, and nonthreatening self, helping him keep his own cool and he begins to describe his own perceptions of the situation and his relationships to the people and the organization. You believe in him—that he does have the capabilities that led to the promotion you arranged for him.

Somehow he lost his way; but, you see no reason to believe he has lost the strengths he used to demonstrate in his work as a sales man. If he is confused, you will help him find his way out of the confusion. If he is frightened by the responsibilities you assigned to him, you'll take it from there. If he is having personal problems, you will make him aware that he has been allowing them to color his on-the-job personality, and that he has not been demonstrating the careful, thoughtful, analytical, and constructive approach to sales and people of which you know he is highly capable. From your own successful years of dealing with people-oriented situations, you know that recognition of the existence of a problem is the first important step to resolving the problem.

E.   On the other hand, a more direct approach is sometimes very productive. Leaning on your maturity and good relationship with Burning-Deck, without apparent anger or irritation, you will tell him that he has been estranging himself from his sales people, letting emotion influence his decisions and his interpersonal relationships. You will share with him your perception that he has been vacillating on important matters and making some imprudent, panicky decisions lately. Warmly, you will suggest he see a personal counselor, perhaps a psychologist or psychiatrist—soon, so everyone can benefit from his rapid improvement.

DISCUSSION OF OPTIONS (PRO AND CON)

Because you are ultimately responsible for the overall performance of the sales department and its component sales districts, and because you are a good manager, you must find the cause of the district's disappointing performance. Assumptions can be quite inaccurate. The feedback you get from the grapevine may be the product of jealous or nonconstructive minds. People gossip and may spread malicious rumors. The effective sales manager is always on guard to assure that he is influenced by facts and not fiction.

It is essential for you to get the facts. Perhaps you have lost touch with the specific district, its customers, geography, and unique characteristics. Did you install a bright salesman in a spot that was tougher than you realized? Did you then leave him too much alone, to sink or swim?

In your search for the separation of fact and fiction, review the reports and records for the past six months to a year. They should reveal facts that have a strong bearing on the present. Perhaps the district was already in deeper trouble than you were aware of when you put the man now called Burning-Deck in charge. Possibly, he inherited a hopeless situation or one that neither he nor you could have handled without special expert assistance. Maybe you thrust him into a group of "sour grapes" rivals, each of whom thought he or she should have gotten the promotion you gave to Burning-Deck and they are now doing their best to dig a deep hole for him. It has happened before and only the most experienced and highly seasoned veterans usually survive and come out on top of this kind of thing.

But, let's look at how Burning-Deck has responded and handled the situation. You may find that he does procrastinate in making decisions, delaying them until he is forced to take positions which often seem hasty and ill-considered. He has become irritable and too ready to pass blame rather than provide support. Clearly, he has not gained the loyalty and backing of his own sales people. The dip in their attitude toward the job matches the sales curve. There probably is a correlation in cause and effect between the two undesirable phenomena. It is your style, one of the reasons for your own growth, to find positive no-lose resolutions to such problems as this one. You have at least the five options described above, and no doubt there are more. But, from among these five, which option enables face-saving while also giving the best promises for long-term benefits? Let's discuss them.

A.   This is the autocrat's way of handling things. In fact, this option, if exercised, concludes that you believe the grapevine, rumors, and gossip. You have already decided the cause of the problem. You have already laid the blame on Burning-Deck and you are not *asking* for cooperation in solving the problem. You are *demanding* it and threatening some undefined but dire consequences if it isn't forthcoming within *your* time frame. High achievers rarely behave like draft animals, twisting and turning in directions forced upon them by a cracking whip. This could enhance the chaos that already threatens the department.

B.   This option adds insult to the injury of Option A. Humanly, it is almost impossible for anyone to readily admit that he is the one at fault in a complex situation, especially when his personality as well as his job performance are the subject of all sorts of nasty accusations. And, it would be unreasonable to expect a 180-degree change just because you demand it. Ordering a person to "face up to reality" is more likely to have an effect that is exactly opposite to the one desired. This option, which is unfortunately very attractive because of its directness, is not quite realistic and smacks of emotionalism. If you feel a person is behaving illogically or emotionally, and if your feelings are accurate, a scolding from the boss is only going to make matters worse. It's good that you reviewed this as a possible option, but even better that you have discarded it.

C.   Cop out, cop out! Calling in the marines could precipitate a major conflict by putting Burning-Deck completely on the defensive. Do it and you can only expect Burning-Deck to go underground, becoming devious and perhaps even less communicative and more withdrawn than before. His sense of insecurity will become intensified. (We all have feelings of insecurity; some are more apparent or visible than others in this regard.)

Bringing in an outside consultant has to be handled with great care when you are doing attitudinal studies of your people. There can be inferences of "let's find the culprits and villains and get rid of them!" Attitudinal studies of groups, sections, departments, or divisional personnel and managers can produce very beneficial results—if the intent of the study is honestly and clearly explained to the participants in advance, and if the participants and their supervisors willingly agree to take part in a study that will *not* direct blame at any individuals. Be careful here. If any of the sales people, including Burning-Deck, have feelings of guilt in the matter, they might defensively sense an attempt to prove their guilt and overact.

D.   There is no finger-pointing in this option, and you can bet on cooperation. This course of action demonstrates your efforts to be objective and impersonal, possessing a healthy combination of task- and people-orientation. It shows you have a feeling of sharing the responsibility for the present situation and are not looking for a "pigeon" to carry the blame for anything. There is an excellent probability that your district manager will even appreciate your interest and concern for his welfare and future, as well as for the bottom line of sales quota. Your nonjudgmental approach is healthy. You make it quite clear that you and he share the responsibility for defining and solving the problem—after you come to an agreement on exactly what the problem is.

By making it quite apparent that you are encouraging his suggestions, ideas, and thoughts, he will respond in his former way (analytically, prudently, and articulately), because you are satisfying one of the most important of all human needs—personal recognition. Perhaps, he has been feeling very insecure in his new environment. Possibly, you share some responsibility for his insecurity. You have left him alone too much, with new tasks to perform and too little guidance. He has been afraid that his shortcomings would become apparent. He is most sincere in his desire to do a top-notch job, not only to achieve personal satisfaction, but also to demonstrate his appreciation to you for the vote of confidence you gave when you promoted him. But, his motivations and needs have been blocked by certain conditions, some of which have not exactly been under his control.

Your wide-open willingness to work with him in improving his interpersonal relationships and productivity will be quite welcome. Clearly, your attitude is going to help him satisfy his needs as an individual as well as a sales manager. You are setting a model for two-way communications that he can translate quite readily into improvements in his relationships with his sales people. With the approach specified in Option D, the prognosis is excellent for long-term success. But before we close this case, let's take a brief look at the last option.

E. How can you "warmly" tell anyone, even a close member of your family, that he or she ought to see a "shrink"? No matter how close or friendly you have been in the past with Burning-Deck, this is too personal a matter to bring into a business environment. Such a suggestion would probably be received as an intrusion, if not as an outright insult. Enough, said. Go back to Option D.

9 STIFF-FINGERS

His "Written" Reports
Never Get Written

Sales reports of bookings and shipments prove that this sales man is one of your top producers. Other pluses include the fact that he is creative, popular, and a super problem-solver. He is almost—not quite—but *almost* the ideal member of your sales team. So, what's the problem here? You'll get some idea of the nature of the problem from his nickname—*Stiff-Fingers.* The problem is with written reports or, more specifically, the lack of written reports. What's wrong with these reports? Well, for one thing, they are never delivered on time. On time? If you do get them at all it's only because you've nagged him to the point where it has become embarrassing to you as well as to him.

THE NEED FOR ALL THE FACTS

There's more. The reports are shining examples of brevity—they're not *concise,* mind you, but just *brief* to the point of being cryptic, rarely containing useful information. If they contain data, and sometimes they do *appear* to contain facts, they read more like "hints," with the facts inadequately substantiated. You hesitate to build your sales plans and forecasts on the basis of the way his "field intelligence" is presented to you. Do you think this is all? Invariably, because he is late in getting reports to you, he has to write them by hand (there's no time to get them typed up) on any convenient scrap of paper (he is always unable to find the report forms), and his handwriting (call it "penmanship") is not exactly readable! Is all this deliberate?

This is not just an *ego* thing with you. You have quite a few reports to read and some of your own to deliver every week, both written and oral. These go to management, and in them you discuss the performance, problems, opportunities, and risks you've dealt with in the past week (as a manager of a sales group) and how you view the short-term and mid-term future. You don't invent these reports. You provide the information and forecasts on the basis of the data, statistical probabilities, and other intelligence contained in the field reports which you receive, read, and carefully analyze.

Aggravation and personalities aside, the lack of timely, informative reports from Stiff-Fingers is beginning to interfere quite seriously with the preparation and accuracy of your own reports. You have always faced, quite squarely, and accepted the fact that comprehensive reporting is part of the job you accepted when you became the sales manager. The system, that is, the organizational procedure which you feel you must accept, requires you to deliver data, your analysis of the data, and your recommendations.

Nobody really *likes* to write reports, especially when they have to be done weekly. Sure, it seems that just as you finish one report you have to start another. This is the way of corporate life; and, it's the life of all people who work in a hierarchical structure. Reports must be meaningful, timely, intelligible, and useful.

An interesting fact is that other members of the group who are less effective than Stiff-Fingers in sales productivity are more, shall we say, "cooperative" in writing and delivering their reports to you on time. You are embarrassed and fed up with having to nag Stiff-Fingers constantly. You are frustrated by the fact that all your efforts have failed to gain the desired effect. The time has indeed come for you to do something in a more direct way that will, once and for all, solve this problem—and keep it solved. You really can't afford to either lose Stiff-Fingers or to allow this difficult situation to continue. You have given it considerable thought and examined your options. You are ready to discuss them with your own supervisor and gain his support for action.

THESE ARE YOUR OPTIONS

A.   He is a top producer in sales. Perhaps you should not try to make a "writer" out of him. Are you, perhaps, being too demanding, too much of a perfectionist, and too much of a conformist? Stiff-Fingers is creative and, like most creative people, he is somewhat of an individualist or nonconformer. He "listens" to a different "drumbeat." In many ways, he does set standards of performance for the rest of the group. Do you think you can learn to live with the situation as it is and accept it as one of the less pleasant burdens of being a sales manager?

B.   How about a middle-of-the-road approach? Perhaps you don't need all the reports in writing. Maybe Stiff-Fingers could be required to give you his reports *verbally*—and *you* could include the information you get from him in your own reports. Or, perhaps, you can settle for one or two of the most crucial reports and let Stiff-Fingers skip all the rest. (For example, voucher-supported expense reports cannot be skipped over.) And, you must continue to have them *promptly* so you have reasonably up-to-the-minute knowledge of the status of your budget. As far as the weekly sales-call reports and his week-in-advance itinerary reports are concerned, both of which you need for sales forecasting and territorial planning, you could provide Stiff-Fingers with a dictating machine into which he could "talk" his call reports and itineraries. Then, he could mail you the cassettes and you could have one of the people in the steno-pool transcribe the information for you. The report forms aren't very long, so his tape-recorded reports shouldn't take too much time to transcribe. And, they would be legible!

C.   You have been very patient and have put up with quite a bit of Stiff-Fingers' behavior and rugged individualism. He will have to play by the rules. How can you justify an exception for him, especially when everybody else follows your instructions? It is time for a serious talk with Stiff-Fingers! You will tell him, just once more, that written reports are *not optional*—they are *mandatory*. If he continues to ignore your policies and practices, this behavior will most certainly be noted in his performance reviews. This could affect his future growth in the company. Put him on notice *right now*. Make it perfectly clear that you are giving him a time limit within which he must conform to the rest of the group as far as timing and completeness of his activity reports goes. You will not mention anything that sounds like "or else" because you don't like to give ultimatums to anybody. But, you will show him your *tough* side quite clearly.

D.   You will determine the reason(s) for this behavior that has earned him his nickname. Is the cause of the problem a conflict between you and Stiff-Fingers, a conflict with the system (also called the "establishment"), does he have some sort of internal conflict, or some kind of hangup about writing? Other than this problem of reports, you and he do communicate well and without stress. Perhaps the two of you can get together. You can then make him aware of how you really feel about the situation and suggest that you and he work closely together toward the development of a practicable solution that will not interfere with what he really likes to do most of all and which he does so very well—*selling*. This appeal will simultaneously enable you to meet your own commitments to management—*planning, organizing, directing, setting performance standards, measuring performance against the standards, and solving problems.*

DISCUSSION OF OPTIONS (PRO AND CON)

Some people view paperwork and the need to prepare periodic reports as symbols of authority and attempts to control their minds. Dramatic as it may sound, this is not an unusual characteristic of creative people who feel they must fight or, at least, oppose such "intrusions" on their exceptionally strong sense of independence. It is important to recognize that such a possibility exists as an explanation of Stiff-Fingers' lack of responsiveness to your requirement for paperwork. Consciously or subconsciously, he may be fighting against your authority—not necessarily against you personally, but against the symbols that are inherent in the requirement to submit activity reports. It's the system, the hierarchical order, and the establishment against which he might be rebelling. ("Nothing personal, boss!")

Then, again, he may be coming from a totally different direction. Perhaps the guidelines set up for reporting—who, when, how, what, and especially *why*—may not be as clear to him as they are to you. Possibly, they are not quite clear to others in the sales group, but they have made assumptions and gone ahead with their paperwork while Stiff-Fingers, being of a more independent mind and more demanding of his leader, has rationalized his resistive behavior. He doesn't like to guess. As with most high achievers, he doesn't like high risks. He wants to *know* exactly what is expected, but perhaps he isn't sure of *what* is expected. So, unfortunately, he does nothing.

It is also possible (and not unusual in a busy sales organization) that he feels his reports are not actually being read, not being used, and not considered meaningful. He may feel, on the basis of experience, that his feedback on competitive activities, customer needs, market shifts, and product mixes is not being read—just date-stamped "received" and then filed. How do such feelings come about? No feedback from the boss, no follow-up calls, no invitations from him to "tell me more about this" can generate the "oh, what the heck" feeling that brings an end to responsible reporting. Where's the responsible *reading?*

Not everyone is an accomplished writer. In fact, you can venture to say that very few people enjoy writing. Go further. Most people dislike having to put their thoughts down on paper. Most people are even lousy letter-writers inside their family environments. For most people, putting on paper all the things that may be going on in their minds can be quite an odious chore. These feelings could be especially strong with Stiff-Fingers. He may have known this from his school days when every essay assignment was a sleep-robbing, agonizing experience. Possibly, he's a good creative writer. But, a factual or documentary-type of assignment as exemplified by call reports, itinerary reports and field forecasts, could reveal a serious weakness among his many skills.

You must also examine another possibility, one which the academic world has only recently begun to recognize and, in a very low-key way, has begun to institute corrective or remedial action. Stiff-Fingers knows his handwriting is illegible and it embarrasses him quite seriously. His school-teachers openly nagged and criticized him for his painfully slow scrawl. Instead of understanding and remdial help, all he got was threats and poor grades. If this little scenario is accurate, he is not fighting the system and has no conflict with you. His fight is an internal one. The last thing he wants to do is recreate the past and relive those misunderstood schooldays. He doesn't want to be hassled. He is willing to and can stand on his field performance.

It's tough on you, isn't it? You're not a psychologist, neither by training nor inclination; nor are you a priest, minister, or rabbi. But, one thing (among many others) which a sales manager must be is a *spiritual* leader (not a *religious* leader) who provides inspiration (call it "motivation"), direction (call it "leadership"), and compassion (call it "understanding").

Whether Stiff-Fingers is "fighting" you, the system, or himself, you must develop and choose the way that offers the greatest promise of solving the problem with long-term benefits to all who are involved. How did you select from among the options that were offered to you? On what basis did you make your selection or rejection? Let's examine them one at a time.

A.   You certainly can't let the situation continue with Stiff-Fingers neglecting his paperwork while all other members of the group properly prepare and submit their reports without complaining. You can't institute a double standard and risk alienating those who do meet their paperwork obligations. You do need the information from *every* member of the team—without exceptions. Creating an exception could be interpreted as favoritism, which is not good management. If you make a concession to one, you must make it for all by changing the rules of the game. Everybody is busy selling in the field and, to all dedicated sales people, the requirement for writing reports may be odious. But, it is accepted and it is fulfilled; it comes with the territory. Making an exception for Stiff-Fingers would, no doubt, solve the problem—but, at the same time, would most likely create other problems that could be worse. There has to be a better way to go.

B.   Where's the "compromise?" You would be doing the "giving" while Stiff-Fingers is doing the "taking." If you do this for him, how can you refuse to do it for others in the group who ask for equal consideration? If your secretary can find time to do Stiff-Fingers' paperwork, how do you get all your other work accomplished? You need a *full-time* secretary, don't you, because of your very heavy workload? Should you give it to the "pool"? Before long, you will have complaints from your peers when their work is being delayed because you have given work to the pool that should be done in the field. If you are willing to omit some of the reports, perhaps you should reevaluate all the reports you expect from the sales people. Perhaps some of them aren't really necessary. They may have been necessary at one time, but "times" do change and so do priorities. Don't give a "lollipop" to just one member of the team. No matter what the final outcome of this situation, you resolve to reexamine your requirements for reports. But, let's continue our search for the best option.

C.   The delivery of an ultimatum always results in a *win-lose* condition. If you were bluffing when you gave an ultimatum to Stiff-Fingers and he calls your bluff, he'll continue as before. He wins, you lose. Another possible reaction is that he might regard the ultimatum as a personal affront, feeling he has lost face and dignity. This reaction can "turn him off," could reduce his motivation, and his productivity could fall off quite significantly. If he accepts the ultimatum as a challenge to his individuality, he could respond by "engaging" you in a personal battle which would manifest itself by an open refusal to accede to your demands (call them "instructions"), or even by speaking out in a deliberately hostile manner in the presence of his peers or of your own supervisor. These attempts to salve his own ego would be at the expense of your ego. This option could lead to a wide open and hostile conflict between the two of you. You might be compelled to fire him for outright insubordination or he might feel compelled to quit to protect his own delicate ego. This is clearly a *lose-lose* situation in which nobody wins. But, your competitor who hires him may find an appropriate solution. Then, who "wins" and who "loses"? The answer is obvious. Please move on to the next option.

D.   Well, you consider yourself to be an accomplished problem-solver and people-motivator. The long-range solution to this particular problem will surely test your skills. You have to give up all conjecture about Stiff-Fingers' behavior. You always deal with facts in your work as a sales manager, and you resolve that you will replace as much conjecture as you can with facts. You will determine the basic cause(s) of Stiff-fingers apparent unwillingness to tackle the paperwork requirements of his job. You will do this in such a simple way that it may not be the obvious way. You will—without anger, resentment, or threats—ask him to try to *describe* the way he *feels* about the paperwork you have asked him to do.

You will be an "active listener," responding positively and not arguing with his statements. He will probably reveal his innermost thoughts during such a discussion—provided you don't turn him off by arguing with him and defending your position as manager. You are in a learning mode. He is, for the moment, the teacher. If he expresses anger, and he might, you must control your own temper. Encourage him to go on and air his feelings without fear of censure from you. He may have something to teach you, despite your seniority in rank. In all likelihood, this is the first real chance he's ever had to express these views. End this discussion with a list of *causes* which are the basis for his behavior, but do *not* list the *effects* of the causes. They are the *behavior* symptoms that you have adequately discussed. Plan a second session in which you will both discuss a program, to which he will make contributions, that will correct the situation without creating a new set of problems for either him or you.

If Stiff-Fingers has been fighting you as a symbol of authority, you will help him understand the work-role you play within the organization. If your management style has been offensive to him, you will explain how that style operates— and you will accept his comments as being helpful, constructive, and worthy of making you look at your own behavior more critically.

If Stiff-Fingers has been fighting the reports because he doesn't believe they make a contribution and take him away from the one thing he understands and does well—*selling*—the burden is clearly on you to improve your communications with the entire sales group. You must make them fully aware of how each of the reports fits into the operation as an important management tool. You will make two promises: (1) you will reevaluate all the reports and forms with an eye to elimination and simplification, and (2) you will not merely read them but will provide feedback on an individual and group basis to verify that the information is actually put to good use. You will help him understand the system (how and why it works), so that he will work *with* instead of *against* it.

If Stiff-Fingers has been fighting himself, defeated by his handicap as a writer, or embarrassed by his poor penmanship, his self-esteem needs bolstering. You will let him know that you have the highest regard for him as a person as well as as an effective sales person. Lots of people are in the same poor-writing boat. You will help him find ways to improve his writing (penmanship) skills. Many adults have overcome the same problem with guidance and practice. You might suggest he learn to type, by taking an evening course at a local adult school or community-college. If he feels he lacks report-writing skills, you can help him by sponsoring his attendance and participation in seminars and workshops on business-report writing. In fact, you will offer the same opportunity to the entire sales team. Then, *everybody* wins!

Whatever combination of approaches described in Option D you elect to take, Stiff-Fingers and you will have, together, acknowledged and defined a serious problem and will have generated a series of solutions that are clearly *win-win*. Now, you can develop a series of specific actions that have an exceptionally high probability for success. You and Stiff-Fingers have reached consensus. And this is vital to success.

While Option D involves a large portion of your time, you will demonstrate to your sales team, to your own supervisor and (just as important) to yourself that you are, indeed, a *good* manager—one who can *give* as well as *take*. Your esteem will expand, your team will increase its loyalty to you and to the company, and everyone's expectations will rise to new high levels. Your company will take special note of your positive skills in solving people-problems.

Go with Option D, of course!

10 SEAT-OF-HIS-PANTS

He Can't—
or Won't—
Plan Ahead

Many top-notch sales people started as part-timers, making extra money after school, between semesters, or during the summer. Some started this way because they weren't sure sales was the career path they wanted to follow—not without first "trying it on." Others went at it full bore by getting into sales full-time right out of school. Do you recognize yourself as one of these? It was exciting looking at the world from the start-up position. There was nowhere to go but up, so to speak. You were one of those who did go up, making it close to the top in fact.

What a wonderful education you gained on the way from field sales to manager! You wouldn't trade it for anything else you can think of. You started at ground-zero, hit the ground running, and gained solid knowledge and practical experience in how a company's hierarchical structure performs.

PLANS AND MORE PLANS

Maybe "performs" isn't exactly the right word to describe the complex, but vital, inter-personal and "inter-thing" activities that go on in any normal business operation. Possibly one of the most important and valuable things you learned from experience and from observation is that every manager you could conceivably call "effective" or "good" had one characteristic in common—they were *planners!* They planned ahead. Oh, things did not always go according to plan, but, at the very least, they had clearly defined and detailed action plans ("road maps"). They had *short-term plans* that measured events in weeks or months, *medium-term plans* that dealt with six months to a year-and-a-half into the future, and *long-term plans* that went farther out into the future than either of the first two kinds.

You learned that the company had a *master plan,* a document that was the amalgamation of all the sub-plans from the individual sectional, departmental, and divisional centers. This master plan was truly the name of the game in which you and all your superiors, peers—and now, your subordinates—participated. Even though you never did get to personally see the master plan, you did know it was a dynamic document, continuously being revised, reviewed, and updated. How was this process accomplished? You knew that when your superior appeared to be probing by asking questions about the future—as you saw it—he was collecting data, opinions, facts, and all sorts of useful information on which to base his contribution to the master plan.

At each level within an organization, there must be an internal kind of plan of action. Every manager has his own name for it. But, typically, sales managers refer to it as a "sales plan" for their particular spheres of responsibility and accountability. In such a plan, objectives are defined, strategies are declared, and programs are spelled out in explicit terms. Timing, personnel, territories, performance levels, and the standards by which individual and group performance will be measured are all detailed and "notched" so as to fit neatly into the master plan.

You learned your lessons well. And, one of the "good manager trademarks" of which you are rightfully proud is your ability to plan thoroughly—and on a timely basis. It isn't easy to do this part of the job. But, if this part is treated lightly, well, you know that luck had better be on your side.

Now, of all people, how could this be happening to you? One of your new field sales managers for whom you had the highest hopes is hard to pin down to specific objectives. In fact, "hard" puts it quite modestly. He's become downright impossible in the area of planning. For example, you ask him for forecasts for his territory for the next year. He comes back, and not too swiftly, with a single number. There is scarcely a bit of data to support the number—strictly "bottom line" numbers; nothing "above the line" is volunteered to support the data.

It is becoming embarrassing, not to mention the fact that it shouldn't be necessary, for you to repeatedly go back to him for the details that support his "total for the period." Without this data—which includes activity by specific account, sales person, product or services to be sold, and an expense budget, all neatly laid over a time base—there is very little credibility. You can't include his bare-boned numbers in your department's or division's plan. And, where is his field plan that tells how the numbers are going to be made to happen? Does he use a rabbit's foot?

This isn't the first time he's done this. By now, you are "up to here" with his evasiveness and delays. You've had it with unfulfilled promises. And, perhaps even worse, you've been burdened once too often by accepting his last-minute forecasts that turn out to be wildly inaccurate when placed against the actuals.

You hate to admit it but you have to—the guy apparently flies or manages by the seat-of-his-pants. You find you refer to him in conversations with your assistants and secretary as Seat-of-His-Pants. This is cute, amusing, and funny for a very short time. You look more closely into the guy's mode of operation and, although you are not surprised, you are quite dismayed to discover the accuracy of the nickname.

He doesn't do anything, so it seems, with advance planning. His sales meetings are called without adequate advance notice. Meetings are announced with: "Hey, you guys and gals! Need to have a sales meeting right away! Come on, please." There is no advance notice of specific topics, to give others time for proper preparation for discussion and presentation of information. He is always out of basic supplies, such as sales-call forms and lost-sale reports (and, there have been too many lost sales lately); even order blanks seem to disappear without being reordered for stock. You can't blame the office secretary for this. He never even set up a procedure to offset shortages of basic materials—that takes *planning!*

He is a likable and popular guy. He sure was one heck of a productive sales person before you made him a field sales manager. But, his sales people are becoming frustrated by him and his ways. Is it *unwillingness* or *inability* to do anything on a planned basis? If he were as effective a manager as he was a sales person, he would be on top of the world, moving rapidly up the management ladder within the company. He declares this is his personal objective. But, he sure is going about it in the wrong way. Something has to be done about this right away. He's having a bad effect on your own work. Guess who's going to do something about it—*you!*

THESE ARE YOUR OPTIONS

A.   You might reassign him to another sales position, or even transfer him to another territory, just to help him save face. Perhaps you promoted him to his level of incompetence. You can't blame him for that, really. Then, again, you are usually right about spotting native talent and that's why you promoted him in the first place. But, you can't take time to experiment. Perhaps you would actually be doing him a favor by relieving him of managerial responsibility. Yes, put him back where he belongs, out in the field with sales accounts and a valuable territory of his own.

B.   Consider the merits of doing the planning for him. You could take care of advance notices and the organization of field sales meetings. Try a sharing situation in which you distribute some of the duties among the field sales manager's subordinates. Set up the internal procedures in the field office for keeping supplies always in stock. Not a bad idea— and also a means for giving some much-needed recognition to other good people in the sales group. And it could help eliminate some of the frustrations you've noticed. You will have your planning done on time and with good supporting facts and documentation.

C.   A good heart-to-heart talk with your field sales manager in the presence of some of the more senior sales people seems in order. You will lay the cards on the table, nicely and politely of course. Seat-of-His-Pants will continue to be responsible and accountable for the planning, but the seniors in the group will do the forecasting and budgets and make certain that things are being done on time and with greater accuracy.

D.   Do you remember whether or not you took an adequate amount of time to fully explain to Seat-of-His-Pants all the responsibilities of the field sales manager and exactly what it is you expect of him? Have you taken time to coach him periodically? There could be two factors at work here: (1) he doesn't fully realize the need or the vital importance of advance planning, and (2) he doesn't quite grasp the technique of how to go about doing it. Why not set aside some time for a calm and cool discussion with him. Make a fresh start. Some of us don't really learn too well "by doing." Some of us require more direction, at least at the start, than others do.

The very newness of the position may be a bit frightening to him. He is totally confident and valuable in an eyeball situation with a customer. But, the "paper mill" can be, to some people, quite an overwhelming matter. His self-esteem might be suffering quite badly. He could actually be delaying actions because of a personal fear of revealing his ignorance. You could become his mentor and his teacher, demonstrating the things you learned about planning ahead when you were at his level in the organization. Your first judgment of him as sales manager material could still be right. There is a possibility you didn't follow through as you and all good managers should when promoting a subordinate. Perhaps you left him too much on his own. The democratic style that you believe in might have been carried just a bit too far this time.

DISCUSSION OF OPTIONS (PRO AND CON)

It may be difficult to put your finger on the exact cause of the problem with Seat-of-His-Pants. Despite his popularity as an individual, he may not be able to identify completely with the company. He did spend many years, successful years, selling as a "soloist." Or, he may be identifying quite readily with his territory and is trying, without even realizing it, to operate his sales group as a solo-type activity and, as such, is not yet accepting his commitments to the company. You happen to symbolize the company. Or, again, he may just not know how to plan. You do not want to lose him either as a sales person or as a potentially top-notch manager. Notice that you never considered firing him as an option. Score one for you. As you know, there is a better way.

A.   It is a rare person who can, gracefully or with gratitude, accept a reassignment to a lower grade as this certainly would be. How would Seat-of-His-Pants respond to such a move from you, his boss? Embarrassment? Demotivation? You may feel you have no choice in the matter at this time except to remove him from this responsible position. However, if you do, be prepared to replace him as a sales person. If he convinces you that he does want to make it work as a sales manager, consider a variation of one of the options given later on in this chapter. Demotion is a tough pill to swallow.

B.   If you were to do the planning for this one person how do you explain to anyone, including your own superior, why you are doing the work of one of your subordinates. Surely, you need the direct feedback from the field and, because you can't possibly be everywhere, that's why you have subordinate managers in your group. Seat-of-His-Pants is closer to the market and the opportunities than you are. A market situation is quite dynamic and constantly changing. He must do the planning himself. You can't distribute his workload among his subordinates. This is confusing *delegation* with the *distribution* of responsibility. If his workload is to be delegated, he must be the one who does the delegating, not you. Recognizing the need for providing recognition is a sign of an "aware" manager, which you certainly are. Taking the initiative away from your manager by reassigning pieces of this manager's tasks is one way to go—if you don't care whether or not the manager stays with the company. It provides a short-term solution to the problem—very short term. This option does not offer long-term benefits to anyone.

C.   How does one "lay the cards on the table" with a manager in the presence of his subordinates? You might as well put a notice on the bulletin board to the effect that, from this point on, the sales group is being managed by a committee you have selected. Boy, oh boy! What a put-down!

D.   Individual effectiveness builds on a base of high self-expectations and confidence in one's own skills and capabilities. This is why so many of us rely on doing things in ways that are familiar and nonthreatening to us.

It is about time—no, it is the *right time*—for you to have a private, candid talk with your man during which you will make him aware of your perception of his on-the-job performance as a manager. You will take great care not to present yourself as a power-boss who exercises the right to criticize. You will make heavy use of *reactive listening*; that is, you will not apply pressure during the conversation. You will give him complete freedom and opportunity to express himself—to tell you how he feels about the job and his relationship with his subordinates and with you. In reactive listening, you encourage him to speak by acknowleging (without criticizing) his comments and statements. You avoid offering counter-arguments to his comments. You give him room to roam, mentally and vocally. In such an environment, his creative intelligence will once again come forth and a positive solution, beneficial to everyone, will begin to emerge.

You may express your belief that you are in part responsible for the creation of the problem, which you now recognize as a *lack of adequate communications.* You will suggest that you and he work together to put things back on the straightest and most effective track. Without talking down to him, you will carefully explain the planning function that is required of all managers in the company.

He may have the answers, but may not really know the questions that are related to developing plans and strategies as part of advance thinking. Together, set down on paper a list of the kinds of questions that require investigation and answers.

For example, how are the local economy and business conditions in his territory? Is the local economy expanding or contracting? Are customer patterns following the direction of the economy? Are they leading or lagging the economy? Are customers buying, or are they holding purchases in abeyance? What are the customers' inventory levels? When does he think they will start buying again, if inventories are high or low? Are there any new local government regulations that are affecting the market and the buying mood? What are the competitors doing? Are there any new products, terms, and conditions with which he feels he must compete? Is the market growing, static, or shrinking? How can you and the home office provide additional help? What is his feeling about the support he is now getting in advertising, sales promotion, technical assistance, and customer services?

There's a whole string of things he might not have considered carefully, before you pointed them out. After all, from whom was he supposed to learn if the teacher rarely came to the classroom?

This pattern of discussion, conversation, and two-way communication you have now established will probably begin to pay off handsomely. You have given him, actually enabled him to discover, an entirely new approach to doing the planning job. You've enabled him to know where to start. His self-confidence in the role of manager will become stronger in a relatively short period of time. He will begin to practice advance planning techniques of his own that will preclude flying by the seat-of-his-pants in his association with you and, especially, with his subordinates.

And, to assure long-term effectiveness, you and he will get together more often by telephone and in person to review progress and make certain that his own self-expectations match, at the very least, those you have for him. Certainly, go with Option D.

11 THE REPEATER

*He Has the Same
Bad Solution for
All Problems*

If ever there was a person with a one-track mind, you know it now. Don't you ever know it! He's working for you—worse luck. He is, really, one of the hardest working sales people in your whole group; not necessarily a top producer, but somewhat above "adequate" and better than most. "He's gonna kill himself, the way he runs!" has been said so many times about him that this phrase has become a cliché around the office whenever anyone refers to this particular person.

Why do they say this about him? Is it jealousy? Are the others displaying envy toward his results? It can't really be that. He seems to be a reasonably well-liked guy around the sales office; not necessarily popular, but not exactly a loner. On the surface it is a puzzlement, to be sure. Nobody wants him to "kill himself," really. But comments such as these do reveal strong feelings and mixed reactions among his peers.

A LESSON NEVER LEARNED

It doesn't require a degree in wizardry to figure this one out. The whole thing is contained in his nickname—The Repeater. You've noticed, but ignored the behavior pattern that is so neatly described in this nickname. He could be one of your top producers beyond a shadow of a doubt. He might even have the potential to be the top man someday. The statistics are all there to verify this possibility. So, what's the problem? What's bugging everyone and why does it now bug you?

Simple—he has one way and only one way of handling every sales situation. It makes no difference who the customer or the prospect is. It makes no difference what the product or the application is. He tackles every situation, customer, product, and application in exactly the same way. He almost works according to a fixed formula. He's totally inflexible!

This, in itself, may not be all bad. But, it can, if you let it, drive you all the way up the wall to watch a grown man approach every opportunity in exactly the same way. Putting it another way, he takes the same *risks* with each opportunity—without apparent regard or concern for the fact that the last time he handled a similar situation "his way" he fell flat on his face and had to scurry fiercely to recover the business. The basic problem, as far as sales technique goes, is that he has no flexibility in his approach to a task, . . . and it makes absolutely no difference whether or not the approach failed last time. He will doggedly return to the same path each time and follow the same set of actions.

In fact, it seems that he becomes most persistent and tenacious when confronted with a sales problem that is similar to the "one that got away last time!" If his approach didn't work last time, he will let everybody know that next time it will work. Talk about stubborn people, he invented stubbornness. His mind is made up; nothing is going to change it. His mind refuses to consider alternative routes. This is what is bugging his peers, and it is beginning to get to you, too. (He deserves to be called The Repeater.)

As manager of the sales group, you are accountable for "aggregate performance," which is the sum of individual performances. The Repeater, you feel certain, could make a still greater contribution to the aggregate by channeling his energies somewhat differently. The most effective sales people behave more like skilled and competitive fencers rather than like bulldozers. They depend on selective strategies and diverse tactics for their successes, not on brute force expenditures of energy. Your job, as you see it, is to provide guidance and the honing of the "tools" and "weapons" of professional and productive salesmanship. Everyone on your team recognizes your strategic skills and responds positively to your guidance and coaching. Everyone, or so it seems, except The Repeater.

Your only complaint, if it can be called a complaint, is that you sincerely believe The Repeater could make a significant leap upward in his sales productivity—in terms of return on selling time invested—if he didn't have his mind so solidly set all the time, whatever the circumstanes. His response is 100% predictable. Give him one simple problem, or a series of dynamic sales problems, and you know exactly how he would handle any one or all of them. This is not the real world of sales. But it is his world, even though it keeps him from becoming *numero uno* in sales and prevents him from being considered for eventual promotion into sales management.

Was it cocktail party chit-chat that you tuned in on or did Freud actually describe what is called a "repetition compulsion principle"? This is, according to Freud, the tendency to repeat an experience or a behavior that was initially successful; *to form a behavioral pattern that becomes a habit.* Okay so far, but the "kicker" is that the specific behavior or response is *compulsively* repeated as a method of coping with each new situation—even when the method repeatedly results in failure. This repetition compulsion may not yet be identified as a "disease," as is compulsive gambling or even alcoholism. But, the results sure do bear a strong resemblance. The more the compulsive gambler's "system" fails, the more stubbornly he is driven to repeat it. It is almost as though Freud had observed your man at work and, through this observation, evolved the repetition compulsion principle.

In the interest of advancing the aggregate performance of the group and, because it is your style to help your people grow in their profession and advance within the company—for your own benefit as well as theirs—you must find a constructive way to deal with (i.e., modify the behavior of) The Repeater. His work pattern and his approach to problem solving must be revised.

What are your options and which one of them holds the greatest promise for long-term success?

THESE ARE YOUR OPTIONS

A.   Is The Repeater carrying habits from his early childhood over into the adult world? Psychoanalysis, which delves deeply into his past, can take years of diligent effort with no promise of success. Psychotherapy might bring about some behavior modification. However, you are neither a licensed psychiatrist nor a trained psychotherapist—nor do you have time for such programs. Your performance is measured at the bottom line, in units or dollars against a base of time. That's the way you should measure this sales person's effectiveness. He's producing at a fairly respectable rate. You only *think* he could do better. Live with it, count your blessings, and leave well enough alone. And, tell the rest of the critics in the group to "cool it."

B.   The "carrot approach" to sales people is often very effective in improving quantitative performance. Hold an inspirational contest; in fact, hold it periodically. By "inspirational," you really mean creative sales techniques. Offer a series of prizes for the most novel ideas for improving sales—

an *idea-of-the-month contest.* The prizes don't have to be elaborate. Recognition is one of the most important awards a manager can give to his sales people. Perhaps The Repeater will get turned on by this concept and begin to open his mind, joining in the fun of exploring new ways to do old things. This approach could have some very exciting side benefits—others on the sales team who are creative would be stimulated. No losers here!

C.   Where there is a "carrot" there is often also a "stick" approach. You are definitely not running a kindergarten. Start stepping in (and, if you have to, stepping *on* this sales person) each time you get a signal that says "here he goes again!" Step in and demonstrate how you would handle it if you were in his place. Give him a detailed description of what you see as the best way to handle his specific customer accounts and prospects. Remind him, in the plainest possible terms, that many people are relying upon him to succeed, that he'd be well advised not to repeat things that didn't work before, and that he'd be wise to try something new or different—at least some approach that does not have a history of failure! Tell him, in case he doesn't know, what his nickname is and how he earned it.

D.   There are ways to tell people unflattering things about themselves that do not necessarily involve *shock treatment.* It is not your style to hurt or cause ego-injury to your people. Sure, you sometimes feel like a school teacher. However, you were most likely advanced into sales management not only because you were a superior sales person, but because you also had the ability to share your special knowledge and skills with your peers and subordinates. You are a talented communicator—not just good with words, but able to deal with abstractions as easily as with the day-to-day pragmatics of bringing in the bookings. Well, you will put your knowledge and experience directly to work on this situation.

You will have a private conversation with The Repeater. Oh, of course, you often have private conversations with him; but this one will be a bit different. He will actually do most of the talking. You will guide the dialogue in this direction by enabling him to review for you a number of his accounts, some of those which he has acquired and developed and some of which he may have lost or dropped. As a reactive listener, one who gives undivided attention to the speaker and does not interrupt with negative comments, you will make him appreciate the time you are giving to him for a private chat. He will probably talk openly about the ones that "got away." This will provide you with an opportunity to go quite deeply into the reasons why they got away—most likely because of his repetition compulsion and inflexibility of style. From here, you move into a discussion of what he might do to prevent recurrences of failures and to increase his "hit-" or "close-rate."

DISCUSSION OF OPTIONS (PRO AND CON)

Remember, one of the functions of a sales manager is to solve problems. The *effective* sales manager solves problems in ways that do not create losers. The effective manager does not overtly take sides in any disagreement among his subordinates. He analyzes the root cause(s) and guides his people in ways that make them feel they are discoveirng new things about themselves, their personality traits and professional characteristics, their on-the-job performances, and their unique and private needs; all the while they are acquiring new skills and improving the capabilities they already have. Through this self-discovery process, they are also able to examine alternative routes that have high probabilities for improvement or correction. With the nonthreatening guidance of the sales manager, they are able to evaluate the options and make the best choice that is suited to the situation. Thus, they are also committed to making it work. They "own" the problem and, therefore, will not usually try to slough it off or pass along any blame as an ego-defense mechanism.

Remember, also, that the easiest way out of a problem for any manager is to fire the individuals who are responsible for it. We've talked about the extreme undesirablity of this approach to problem solving—or this "non solving" approach to problems. So, again, in this situation, we want to keep our team intact while improving interpersonal relationships and, of course, enhancing productivity. It is now time to examine the pros and cons of the options available for this situation.

A.   This option is not all bad. If you are the kind of manager who operates on the basis of "let nature take its course," this should be especially attractive to you. However, as you learned in another case study, the laws of nature tend to become perverse. This is akin to gambling rather than managing. If, as a problem-solver, all one had to do was let nature take its course, fewer managers would be needed in any organization. Anyone can just sit back and let things happen by themselves. This is a management style also known as "rubbing the rabbit's foot." (Don't bother going to the library; you won't find any mention of this as a formal style in any textbook on management or leadership, although some do refer to it as "abdication.") The risks are high—too high. "Living with it" is an expensive luxury the effective manager recogizes he cannot afford. You must maximize or optimize individual productivity. Unless you are the sole owner of the company, you do not have the authority to speculate with the company's resources. In your area of accountability, sales people are a company resource; you must manage the resource, not live with the problem.

B.   Incentive programs, when properly timed and implemented, can be good tools for increasing an individual's selling efforts. However, such programs usually produce short-term effects. And, consider this probability: The Repeater will work as hard as anyone else—but, *in his same old*

way. No, this will not bring about the desired behavior modification. More likely, it will reinforce the *modus operandi* you
are trying to get rid of.

C.   This smacks of the use of power based on authority
and rank, rather than on *knowledge.* If you start "stepping in"
or "stepping on" one of your people, rgardless of how his
peers view him, you will create an underdog relationship
that will win sympathy for The Repeater and an undesirable
nickname for you. Furthermore, if, as you believe, he is a
high-achiever type, he will innately be an individualist. Constantly standing behind and looking over an individualist's
shoulder is virtually guaranteed to turn him off! This option
is super-charged with backfire possibilities—with you standing directly in line with the backfire. Not only are there no
winners here, *you* could be the loser!

D.   Now that we have gone through Options A through
C, it becomes obvious that option D has the best probability
for success. This is an adult approach to problem solving,
one in which logic prevails and emotions are controlled.
Note that we said emotions are "controlled," although they
are not necessarily "eliminated." Our friend, The Repeater is
operating from an emotional base of ego-defense. Influenced
by parents, family, friends, and teachers during the years
when his personality was being formed, he needs (although
he may not be aware of the need any more than he is aware
of his repetition compulsion) the guidance and direction of
someone he respects and who can provide the logic he is not
able to bring to bear on his conduct. Your task is to do this.
Note, however, that it is not said or implied that you should
take on the role of the parent; he's probably had an overkill
of parenting. If he were to sense you were trying to be his
"daddy," he would very likely argue with and consider your
view to be a personal intrusion rather than as a series of
much-needed asists.

Option D establishes a new level of relationship that is
fully positive. The direction you are coming from is one of

knowledge, rather than "power" or hierarchical rank. You are being nonjudgmental, examining data, looking at facts, and assessing the present on the basis of history. Both of you are moving together toward an analysis and resolution of the problem, effectively elminiating risks and creating opportunities. He will recognize, without having to be told, that some of his products and accounts may have been getting inadequate or inappropriate attention—as a result of his repetitious behavioral tendencies. Don't expect sudden, miraculous changes. For a while longer, The Repeater will repeat his past performances. However, by agreeing on a series of benchmark conversations in which he can candidly review his (and your) perception of progress with you, he will take charge of himself and in good time move to a new, higher plateau of performance. His self-perceptions will be enhanced. His self-expectations will be increased. He will recognize the value of modifying his own behavior. He will learn and develop an important new set of skills—new approaches to old situations that will increase his success rate as measured by any set of sales-manager's arithmetic. And, you will become more highly regarded by your peers, subordinates, and superiors.

How about your own self-esteem? Going up!

12 THE STRANGULATOR

He Gets All Tied Up
in His Own "Red Tape"

You've met this one before and will probably meet him again. Look closely at the mirror and determine whether or not you fit the description. (It's never too late to learn.) "This one" is the sales manager or sales supervisor, usually called a "boss" with no compliment intended, who does everything *by the book!* He has a rule, often called a "policy," for just about everything. If there is no rule or policy in existence to cover the specific set of circumstances, he will create one in a jiffy. "Where's my book? Where's my book? Golly gee, I must have left it in my car! Oh, what'll I do now?" This is the grief-stricken cry of the supervisor, manager, or boss who can't or won't make a move without his "book of rules" or "policy manual."

POLICIES, PROCEDURES, RULES AND REGULATIONS

Now, rules and policies are essential to the consistent (not necessarily smooth, but consistent) operation of any group activity. They establish, or are intended to establish, ground rules, boundaries, guideposts, and codes of conduct that apply to all members of the organization. Hardly anyone will challenge the general need for such a document. The cause of concern here is the amount of dependence this particular group leader has on the book of rules or policy manual, which most likely he has written himself in the firm belief that everyone wants to know where he stands and how to conduct himself under a given set of circumstances. Although excellent in its concept, this book of rules makes no allowances for the type of extenuating circumstances that nine out of 10 salespeople encounter on 90 out of 100 calls.

In this case study, working by the book has become a hindrance rather than the help the guy who wrote the book likes to think it is. A little later in this chapter, we will closely examine some of the probable reasons why this supervisor has an overpowering need for such a book and why he panics when he can't put his finger on the right page—the one that covers the way to deal with a specific incident that has come to his attention.

What incident or series of icidents brought this situation to your attention? One indication of trouble was the excessive absenteeism in his group when compared with other sales groups in the department or division. Also, you noted that many of the sales people in this particular group were late in arriving at the office or tended to forget when an internal meeting was called. Oh, they were rarely late for customer appointments; they never forgot one of those, thank goodness! Well, then, why didn't they attach some priority to the need to attend internal meetings or to arrive on time at the office at the start of the day? You've heard some sarcastic comments that half the sales people in this group were probably moonlighting or looking for another job. At first you ignored them; but, you can't ignore anything connected with this specific group because the sales records clearly indicate something negative is happening. There's been a distinct falloff in bookings. And, it correlates with the time you promoted the star sales man in the group to district sales manager.

It's time for you to check it out. You visit the sales office for a review of the matter with your manager. You can't fault his record-keeping; it's impeccable. You can't fault his apparent knowledge of the market and the customers for which his group has sales responsibility; it's thorough. You can't fault the base-pay levels being paid to the sales people. They're equal to or better than the competition's and equitable for the area's cost of living index. Commission rates and bonus plans are the best.

What do you suppose has happened? What has caused what appears to be a group "turnoff?" What has happened to what used to be a highly motivated group of high achievers? The review with your sales manager is taking longer than you had expected, indicating that the cause or causes are not superficial. It does occur to you at first that the manager himself might be the cause or part of the cause. But, some of the things he says and tends to repeat in your conversations now take on a new significance. You ignored them at first because they sounded like clichés, hardly worth thinking about. For example, you heard such comments from him as:

> They (his sales people) seem to enjoy breaking the rules and regulations.
>
> Company policy doesn't mean a thing to them (his sales people).
>
> They (his sales people) want to do just as they please, without rgard for guidelines.

You are now aware of and sensitive to his repeated use of such key words as "they," "rules and regulations," "company policy," and "guidelines." They take on important values now, more important than they did at first. His use of the word "they," instead of the more typical "my sales people," is very different for a sales manager who thinks possessively of his group. This implies a sense of separation between the manager and his subordinates, rather than a "togetherness" with each owning a part of the other. Rules? Company policies? Guidelines? A few questions about the rules and regulations, company policies, and guidelines reveal the cause that has effected the demotivation!

You ask to see a copy of the rules, policies, and guidelines to which he has been referring. Sure enough, he does have such a book; but, with just a few exceptions, you've never seen these before! They are, for the most part, *his* rules, policies, and guidelines and not the company's! *He* created most of them himself.

He's been "strangling" his sales people. Not literally, of course, but the effect has been to "choke off" individual expression, initiative, and motivation. High achievers are, generally, creative people in their fields. Creative people require a certain amount of freedom. They do not respond positively to heavy doses of regulation. Quite the opposite is true. They cannot, of course, be allowed to roam and operate as they feel. The successful team consists of a group of individualists who work toward a common objective. The development of the team is related to the management style of its leader.

You firmly believe that the manager's style is that of an over-regulator—one who binds instead of guides. He apparently is not aware of the fact that he has no authority to make company policy; this comes from levels above your own in the hierarchy. Although his intentions have been to meet the objectives of his position, he is failing. And, his group is failing as well.

All this is history now. On this base of new knowledge, startling though it may be to you, you must implement a program that will restore morale and productivity. You have no reason to doubt your original choice of the person you promoted to manager. However, you may doubt your own wisdom in not having communicated more frequently and more closely with your man—whom you now refer to (privately, of course) as *The Strangulator*. Later on, you will discover that this nickname is quite close to some of those used by the sales people. Yes, some of the fault is yours and you admit it to yourself as the first step toward correcting the situation.

What should you do? How do you get the sales people turned back on without putting down and turning off the highly motivated, although somewhat erroneous, supervisor?

THESE ARE YOUR OPTIONS

A.   Come on strong to offset the weakness of the supervisor. Temporarily suspend all the rules, regulations, policies, and guidelines. Just tell the sales people and the supervisor quite plainly what you expect of them. Then, let them go ahead and get the task done on their own.

B.   Support your local manager! Support The Strangulator because you are the one who promoted him and you are the one who failed to communicate adequately. It would be inappropriate now for you to isolate and lay the blame squarely on him. You will accept no arguments from the sales people when you advise them that you support the rules, regulations, polices, and guidelines. The supervisor is accountable for the success of the district. He is the captain of the team and the members must play the game according to the "plays" as he calls them. In fact, anyone who does not follow the captain's signals will be disciplined.

C.   As an add-on to Option B, you will announce your intention to post the names of rule-breakers on the office bulletin board. You will let the office know that you are giving The Strangulator your complete support. The threat of personal embarrassment and public notoriety might be the way to bring the office back into line.

D.   On the other hand, The Strangulator is probably neither *all wrong* nor *all right*. You propose that both of you review the entire set of rules in his book together. You will discuss the objectives of each of them, analyze the phrasing and implementation, and review their effectiveness individually and collectively. You propose that priorities be assigned to each one and that specific efforts be made to reduce the quantity by eliminating those whose benefits are probably marginal. Your experiences as a manager of people and projects have taught you that people do want and do expect rules, regulations, and guidelines. However, people will accept them only as long as they are reasonable in their intent and quantity, and as long as the manager is flexible in his style as an enforcer.

DISCUSSION OF OPTIONS (PRO AND CON)

Rules, regulations and some controls are essential to the smooth and coordinated functioning of a group of individuals—and this may be especially true of those who tend to operate as "rugged individualists." Controls may serve as effective early-warning signals of trouble or of increases in operating risks that might affect the performance of the group. The "declaration" of rules and regulations by the manager enables the subordinates to develop perspectives with respect to relative values and priorities. On the other hand, as we have observed in this situation, too many controls destroy values and, because of the implication or inference that the individual is not competent to exercise initiative or judgment, all priorities and controls may be ignored and even defied. The members of the group begin to feel they are being strangulated. Positive thinking and the type of creativity that is most effective in a competitive sales environment may diminish or vanish.

What causes a supervisor, even a highly intelligent one, to become so dependent upon a book of rules that he will create one if it does not already exist? There are several possibilities to consider. A severe lack of self-confidence as a decision maker can make a manager dependent upon a book that provides prefabricated judgments. A fear of failure can be diminished by having a book of rules to fall back on—a *crutch,* if you will. A sense of insecurity can be stimulated by poor communications between a supervisor and his manager, in which case the book becomes a sort of security blanket. In fact, all of these conditions can be operating at the same time.

It is important to The Strangulator, to your own growth, to the advancement of the individual members of the sales group, and to the growth of the company that you support your subordinate manager now. It is vital that you make certain that genuine and honest two-way communications exist and are practiced between you and your subordinate manager. You appointed him to the position for good reasons. You can help him overcome his feelings of inadequacy and insecurity, especially if he is a new supervisor who is accountable for the work output of others. You can help him grow in his job, and to overcome this particular hangup. Everyone will benefit, including you. In this light, let's review the effects of the individual options available to you.

A.   Stepping in and taking charge, completely overruling everything that The Strangulator has done, is a clear indication that you do not support your subordinate manager. This would virtually destroy his potential for achievement and would be a poor management example for you to set. The Strangulator might resign, which you do not want. Or, he might stay on, filled with bitterness and resentment, blaming you for interfering with his work and perhaps unconsciously working to prove you are ineffective as a problem-solver. Also, the group will recognize that you do not support your own manager. Furthermore, there is no indication that the group of sales people want to operate as a bunch of free-wheelers. Will any of them cherish or relish the idea of becoming a supervisor who reports directly to you? Not likely!

B.   Disciplining someone who breaks the rules is hardly

likely to achieve the desired effect. After all, we are not in the military services, we have not been read "articles of war." It is generally known by the sales people that The Strangulator has been overdoing things by going strictly according to the book—*his* book. But it is time to apply logic and sweet reason.

C.   This is option is just as inappropriate as B. Everyone has been breaking The Strangulator's all-encompassing rules. You might as well administer mass punishment, making everyone bitter and resentful. This is tantamount to suicide—a permanent solution to a temporary problem.

D.   The supervisor and his sales people are the most important resource the company has given to you as a means for contributing to the achievement of the objectives defined in the company's master plan. They recognize the need for reasonable controls and intelligent administration. They know there is a need for setting standards by which performance can be measured. They also know there is a fine line— hard to define—between "too much" and "just right." In this light and from this perspective, it is very prudent to reexamine the book of rules.

Rewrite, reject, subtract, and add wherever necessary to establish the quantity and quality of rules and regulations at a level that improves the probability that the objectives of the group will be met. As a direct result, the objectives of the company will also be attained. You will go so far as to consider inviting the group to participate in the development of the revisions to the book. Thus, they will have participated in the creation of the standards by which they will be measured. They will feel they are accountable, as well as responsible, for observing the requirements of the book as much as anyone does. This will increase their support and willingness to follow the new rules and regulations, now known as "our book." Yes, Option D offers the greatest probability for long-term success and fulfillment. It will enable you to get rid of the detestable nickname "Strangulator;" and you will prove that your selection and promotion of the supervisor is further evidence of your own exceptional skills as a manager, as a person who can and does develop leaders, and as an effective people-problem solver.

13 RIGID-ROGER

*He Could Be
the Perfect Model
for Resistance to Change*

Most of us dislike changes. Possibly one of the few changes we welcome is a change in salary, bonus, or commissions—provided this particular change is an increase! There are many clichés, and you may have used some of them yourself without realizing they reflect your objection to change. For example, when there is an organization change and people get shuffled around at the managerial level, one may say: "If my boss calls, get his name;" or, "The one thing you can depend on around here is change;" and, "Change is our mathematical constant applied to people." From a German proverb comes the saying "To change and to improve are two different things." From another source, of unknown authorship, we get "Any change, even for the better, is always accompanied by drawbacks and discomforts."

Sigmund Freud is credited with the observation that man is a pleasure-seeking, pain-avoiding animal. He wrote in one of his letters: "I have examined myself thoroughly and come to the conclusion that I don't need to change *much."* The emphasis on "much" is my own because it qualifies the need for change, even as viewed by Freud.

CHANGE CAN CAUSE DISCOMFORT

Departing from the clichés and returning to my own observations as one who has worked extensively with professional sales people and managers at all levels in a diverse collection of industries, I can honestly say that one of the most severe causes of managerial failure is an inability to resolve conflicts within the manager's own areas of accountability—without creating winners and losers. My further observation is that one of the most common causes of conflict is a product of the way change is introduced—call it "managed" or "mismanaged." Review in your mind the things that happened the last time you changed things in your bailiwick. You got a lot of complaints, flack, and feedback, directly or indirectly from your subordinates, didn't you? You had to put a stop to it with the command: "Enough! That's the way it is!" You figured those who didn't like the new way would come around sooner or later. In the meantime, *tough!*

However, the interval during which you waited for the noise level to subside and for things to get back to "normal" was, I don't doubt, very tough on you. It was probably tough on everybody, but too bad. Change, properly managed, doesn't have to be tough on anybody. It doesn't have to generate unmanageable conflicts and it shouldn't put you to a dangerous test. "Ah, but it does," you say, "because not everybody will go along with changes. In fact," you add, "some even actively resist; they work to make the change a big flop! Imagine, some of my own people act as though they are trying to dig a pit for me to fall into!"

Sorry, we can't relieve you of the responsibility for planning and introducing change. It comes with the sales manager's territory. However, we can help you learn to cope successfully with the individuals who most actively resist change. A full treatise on the planning and implementation of change is beyond the scope of this book. However, the following case history is taken from a typical, real-life experience. The details enable you to infer some of the positive techniques and reduce some of the pitfalls inherent in the system known as change.

Every manager, any person who is accountable for the work performed by others, is responsible for implementing changes in the workplace—changes in procedures, territories, organization, people, places, and things. To some degree, if a product or service is involved, the sales manager's field-intelligence can be responsible for causing changes in product or service formats and concepts. And, the person responsible for having created, designed, or manufactured the company's product or service may resist any attempts to change his "pet" from one form into another.

Successful change involves successful negotiation. One would tend to believe that sales professionals are top-notch negotiators; but, such is not necessarily the case under all circumstances. If there is emotional involvement—one pet idea butting up against another's pet—the negotiating skills have a tendency to disappear. They are ineffectually overcome by the powerful influences of human emotions, which are often destructive rather than constructive in effect. Even when one side prevails over the other, there is a period of transition; that is, a time interval during which the changes are being effected. This transitional period is a critical period during which the desired change may be efficiently implemented, truly achieving the desired result, or may be "harpooned," "torpedoed," "destroyed," "defeated," or "killed off." If the manager was the originator or champion of the desired change, he loses. If the desired change was beneficial and desirable, but is defeated, everybody loses. There are no winners!

No doubt, planning and implementing a change in your group, section, department, or division is a significant challenge. It is a responsibility you have accepted with the territory.

Now, it is time for you to put into action a change you have been thinking about for a long time. You've planned it well on paper. To the best of your knowledge, no detail within your purview has been overlooked. Your own supervisor supports it. You've made a firm commitment against a time base for its completion. You've included, as a manager should, benchmarks and quantitative checkpoints for evaluating the effectiveness and merits of the change—which also become, by implication, measurements of your own effectiveness and managerial merits.

For purposes of our discussion, the specific nature of the change is not important to write or read about. The important elements are the methods which you, in the role of this hypothetical manager of change, have used to make it all happen. Let's bring the situation and the problem up to date.

Most of your people, those affected by the change, have gone along with the program. However, there's stubborn resistance from one of your top producers whom you have pointedly and privately nicknamed *Rigid-Roger.*

For obscure and unpredictable reasons, Rigid-Roger is resisting the change. To make matters worse for you, he is complaining long and loudly to all who will (and to some who won't) listen. We emphasize the fact that if he were not one of your top producers, you would arrange a transfer as an attempted solution to this blatant insubordination. But he is, as a sales person, a valuable asset to your own statistically measured performance. You don't want to lose him. But, you sure would like to get him to see things your way. Ah! "See things your (my) way!" Hold that thought for a while. We'll get back to it as we continue. The phrase should refer to *our* way, not *my* way—right? Well, you sincerely believe the change is to everyone's benefit and deserves, therefore, to be given a fair chance. It really is *our* way; *our* change for the better. Sorry about that slip. Call it "semantics" if it makes you feel better. But, it is better to think about *our* group rather than my group; our program rather than my program. More than semantics, it's a managerial attitude that others will clearly perceive. Be careful about that!

Let's get back to Rigid-Roger. His attitude is having a negative effect on his work. Worse, yet, his colleagues are feeling the effects of Rigid-Roger's griping. Whether or not they agree with him the effect on their performance is noticeable. Give the plan—the change—a chance to work, fellows! And, above all, during this period of transition, let's keep sales moving; don't slow down. But, they have slowed down. You realize you must take some action. The finger points clearly at Rigid-Roger. This means you must take some action relating to him, specifically some action that will have long-term benefits. It will, ideally speaking, convert him from a resistor to a supporter, thus enabling the change to stand on its intrinsic merits. Options, please!

THESE ARE YOUR OPTIONS

A.   You might assume that the change has made Rigid-Roger feel insecure. Perhaps you never noticed before that he is basically a very insecure guy. Perhaps that's one of the reasons he is such a hard worker, having to prove to himself as well as to others that he is a competent performer. You've never had a real close personal relationship with him; you're not that kind of manager, which is okay. But, maybe, in this case, you would do well to be a bit more social with a subordinate. Yes, that's it. You will get together with him after work for cocktails, dinner, and a nice chat. You will prove to him the need for the change and how he, as well as the company, will benefit from the whole thing. The old "persuader" in you will do the job right!

B.   There are, in fact, times when the boss just has to get tough about things. You can't water a garden without pressure to force the water from the hose. You will turn on the pressure. There are times when direct approaches are called for. This, you perceive, is a time for directness, with no pussy-footing around and no hinting at things. You will call Rigid-Roger in for a serious talk. You see his behavior as being childishly rebellious and you want him to recognize this fact. You fully expect him to work with, not against, your project. Point out that in such a battle, *he will lose.* You will remind him of your past appreciation for his many valuable contributions to the company (for which he has been well paid) and you will acknowledge your honest desire to keep him on your team (let him infer the threat). Emphasize that you, and you alone, are the manager and are not going to tolerate any disruptive behavior from within the group—regardless of past track records.

c.   Try some theatrics. "Surprise" Rigid-Roger into a more receptive and cooperative frame of mind. Use a combination of humor and shock tactics, amply larded with clichés such as, "You can count on change" or "If you don't like the plan, wait a few minutes and it's sure to change." Rigid-Roger is no fool. He'll get the message and recognize he is nonconforming in his attitude and that his way is a dangerous way to operate. It might just work.

D.   Another course of action is to call a special staff meeting (if the next regularly scheduled one is a long way off) with all of Rigid-Roger's peers attending. Use this as an opportunity to describe the situation that existed before the change was put into effect, the need for making the change, what options were open to you, the pros and cons of each option, and the logic that led to the option that is now being implemented. You will even go so far as to describe any possible weaknesses or negative aspects of the change that is being put into effect. Give everyone at the meeting, especially Rigid-Roger, the opportunity and time to discuss openly and candidly any doubts or questions they may have in their minds. Lay all the cards on the table—face up! This is a real test of your ability to communicate with your group, isn't it? Are you up to this kind of self-test? You can't afford to fail this one. But, it is one option available to you. You must decide.

DISCUSSION OF OPTIONS (PRO AND CON)

What is the fundamental error that was made, unfortunately by the sales manager, from the very start? The sales manager acted alone throughout the process of determining the need for change, for developing the plan, and for putting it into action. The entire activity became *his* plan and *his* program. He fully expected his subordinates to acept *his* plan and *his* timetable without question. But, where was the *ownership* of the entire affair? Certainly not with the group or its individual members.

The fundamental, and very serious, error was the exclusion of his subordinates from the preliminaries.

Note that the manager did seek and obtain the approval and support of his own supervisor. He wanted to be part of his supervisor's thinking and activities. Two-way communications—isn't that what he wanted and got from his own supervisor? However, he did not translate this same need in a downward direction, from the organizational viewpoint. He worked the whole thing out. Handed it to his subordinates as an accomplished fact and then expected them to adopt and support it without question. He may have the right in the hierarchy of his organization to mandate, dictate, and command. However, in an environment of high-achieving professional sales people he would have been very well advised to bring them into the affair from the very beginning. He should have obtained their agreement that there was in fact a need for change; that all would benefit, even though to different degrees as individuals; that the plan for change and its implementation would *belong to all* members of the group.

Ownership is the name of this game. It is entirely possible that some members of the group might have made some suggestions at the start of the analysis and planning (diagnostics) phases, resulting in (1) a better plan, and (2) a plan that would be strongly supported by those directly affected by the implementation of the programs. The Japanese, whose management methods are currently in vogue and much discussed, call this "management by consensus." We don't necessarily recommend carrying it as far as the Japanese do. Our Western style and culture may not tolerate a completely Oriental approach.

All well and good; this is what should have been. But, is it too late? We still have a business to run. Sorry, the sales manager appears to have goofed. Now, how do *you* in the hypothetical role of the sales manager get the "train back on the track?" Okay, next time it will be different. Let's get Rigid-Roger back to doing constructive work; get everybody to concentrate on moving forward. On with the show! Which of the four options offered to you did you choose? Why did you choose it and why did you reject the others? Perhaps you came up with a combination of features selected from among Options A through D. This is perfectly valid. Match your own conclusions against our evaluation of the four proposed choices intended to correct the situation.

A.   Approaching Rigid-Roger on a highly individualized basis has strong backfire possibilities—backfiring on you, that is. The sudden change in your social behavior will put him on guard. You don't want him to go on the defensive with you. However, it is entirely possible and highly probable that he will take everything you are saying as a criticism of his behavior. (Come now, isn't that what you are really doing?) Rigid-Roger, as a top producer, is probably very articulate. When attacked, he might counterattack, and your thoughts of a pleasant and sociable evening can be shattered as you find yourself dueling and sparring with words against a guy who is no amateur player at this sport.

B.   Interesting. You definitely are not Rigid-Roger's "drill sergeant." Yet, if you choose to follow the recommendations of this option, you are certainly behaving like one. If you can't accept the drill sergeant label, accept the proposition that you are behaving in a dictatorial, highly authoritarian way. You demand that he obey your commands! He must cease to challenge and question your decisions and actions! The scenario is also from a low-budget, Western melodrama: "There's not enough room in this town for both of us!" And, in this script you are the "federal marshal" and he is ranked only as a "deputy sheriff." It will probably be eminently clear to him that he is being told: "Time to move on before we have a shootout!" This isn't the solution you are searching for.

C.   Sorry, but this option offers too oblique an approach to problem solving. The point can be missed—totally—as you play "show biz" tactics. The indirectness of the method proposed in this option will probably cause Rigid-Roger to draw his own conclusions as to just what it is you are trying to get at. He may conclude that (1) you have "lost your marbles," (2) you are trying to make a point but never did get to that point, (3) you are criticizing him for something and he doesn't really know what it is, (4) he is being given an indirect order to change his way of doing things but is unclear as to what needs to be changed, or (5) it is time to move to another company where he can feel more comfortable as well as more appreciated. In all probablity, he will know no more about his negative contributions than when he came in. Quite probably he will leave the session feeling demotivated. Of course, none of these responses reflects the desired effect. He's a logical person who comprehends and deals in logical discussion and argument. Don't try the emotional appeal with him that is inherent in this option.

D.   There are, as you know, several type of meetings. (We ascribe to the belief that every meeting should have a defined purpose or objective.) The type of meeting suggested in this option combines two objectives; (1) informational and (2) problem solving. An informational meeting provides all attendees with an excellent opportunity to establish two-way communications (possibly three-way—up, down, and lateral). It may not be too late to collect and share data with your subordinates, updating them on the causes that led to the introduction of change, just what the change that is under way is all about, your expectations from the individual members of the group and from the group as a whole, and what you forecast the impact will be on the future.

This process will invite discussion. You will state openly and sincerely that future changes will involve such discussions with the group *before* they are implemented. (The point you will make is that from now on you are going to ask for ideas, suggestions, and recommendations from your group as *inputs* for the determination of the *need* for change, for the *kinds* of change that will satisfy the need, and the optimum way to bring about any such change.) This will tend to remove any threat posed by the introduction of change in the future. As for the present, your demonstrated willingness to "lay all the cards on the table" and answer all questions with candor has the effect of willingly putting yourself "on the defensive" in front of the entire group. You will not single out anyone, including Rigid-Roger. Neither by implication of statement nor by inference through a fixation of your eyes on any one person while you are speaking will you "point a finger." Rigid-Roger and any member of the group who has heard him gripe, and possibly has been leaning sympathetically in his direction, will have been given a full opportunity to state their views, attitudes, or suspicions. And, you will have been given an opportunity to constructively restore perspectives by removing distortions and fears.

Why not carry this one step further? Ask your group to add the subject of the current change to the agenda for the regular staff meetings at which time all of you will review and evaluate the progress being made by the implemented change. If the group does not report progress, tell them you will welcome their ideas on how to modify or revise the program so that the desired and beneficial effects of the program may be realized.

What do you suppose was Rigid-Roger's personal problem? Really, it was not different from everyone else's problem in the group. He is intelligent and, in his field, a creative person. Such people do not like, in fact they detest, having ideas and changes imposed upon them. They think they can make intellectual as well as physical (sales) contributions to the growth of the group and the company. Recognition is what he wanted. Probably, others in the group felt this need for recognition just as strongly; but, Rigid-Roger couldn't suppress his strong feelings the way others in the group did. It may be difficult to recognize at first that Rigid-Roger, however unintentionally, did you a great service by not concealing his inner feelings but allowing them to surface. You responded appropriately with Option D and his needs have been fulfilled.

Yes, through Option D, you and all your group members will have learned several important lessons concerning the management of change and the reduction of conflict. These include the fact that within an organizational entity, the genesis of cooperation, motivation, and productivity is often derived from group participation in the conceptional as well as implementation phases of plans and programs.

14 YOU-BLEW-IT

Your Sales Contest—
and It Fizzled

You blew it! You blew the whole thing and you didn't know it until it was too late to do anything about it. Your powerful instincts (reinforced by the poor bookings reports) told you things were not going according to plan. You knew you had a problem, but you couldn't define it. Therefore, you couldn't come up with a solution. Give yourself a nickname—*You-Blew-It!*

What brought you to this self-condemning, sad state of affairs? You—the boss and sales manager—have made a serious error. You, too, have lessons to learn and this is a powerful one. We seem to have come in at the middle of this story, so let's go back to the beginning, bring the incident up to date, and then come to a satisfactory conclusion.

EVERY CONTESTANT A WINNER

It all began when the vice-president for marketing and sales (your own boss) asked for a special sales push in the fourth quarter of the fiscal year. He gave you plenty of advance notice so that you could plan an effective strategy and create a program that would have a high probability for success. You did develop an action plan, one for which you had so much enthuisiasm that you made a very strong commitment: If the company would give you an additional 6.5% overlay to your department's promotion budget, you would return a 17.5% incremental contribution to profit.

This was, to say the least, a bold self-challenge. However, you were so confident of success and the performance of your sales people that you put the entire program in writing, as a formal memorandum. It looked good enough to your manager to merit support. The appropriate transfer of funds was made by memoranda to the financial department. Your boss updated the sales plan and made his commitment to the company president. You had (a) the plan, (b) the budget, (c) the motivation, and (d) the sales team that could produce the desired results. Unfortunately, it didn't work. How come?

Take some time for serious reflection and analysis. Review the plan you put together which was intended to produce the desired results.

The basis of the plan, the "motivator," was a series of valuable prizes. So far, a rather ordinary idea. But, this one had a significant twist. There would be no losers, only winners. You learned from past experience that in any contest the same 20% of the team would walk off with 80% of the prizes. In fact, the pattern had become so familiar that anybody in the sales department could name the first-, second- and third-place winners in a sales contest. So, how was this contest different? Well, maybe you didn't invent this particular wheel, but, in your department, the concept was novel. Instead of each sales person competing against the rest of the team, each would compete against his own past record of performance—logical and, on the surface, workable.

The idea was that each sales person would be given the same fixed-percentage increment in quota for the contest period. For example, Jonah Jones in Territory B had a $193,000 quota for new bookings in the fourth quarter. His quota for the period would be increased 20% to a total of $231,000. The same percentage rate of increase would be applied to all territories, regardless of the base quota. Thus, each territory had its own "nut" to crack, independent of all other territories. The awards would be based on relative attainment of percentage of quota. Each sales person would be working toward improving his own, individual performance rather than trying to outperform any other sales person in the department.

Basically, this was not a bad idea. Each of the sales people did develop the data on which quotas were founded. After discussions with you, each had agreed on the number that became the individual's quota for the period. The aggregate of individual quotas (with a "hedge" factor) became the department's commitment or sales plan. This, in turn, became part of the division's commitment to top management. So, you had acted appropriately in developing and assigning individual quotas. Each member of the sales team "owned" his base quota as a personal commitment—a "contract," so to speak, between you and the individual.

Yes, 20% was a big add-on but so were the rewards. The winners would be calculated entirely on the basis of attainment of percentage of personal quota. The greater the percentage of attainment, the bigger the prize. Thus, the sales persons who worked in low-productivity territories (usually sales persons with lesser skills) had as good an opportunity to win a top prize as did the sales persons in the so-called "rich" territories.

And the list of prizes—wow! There were twenty-three sales people in the department and 23 prizes. The top prize was a new luxury car. The bottom prize wasn't at all shabby either—a complete deluxe camera outfit, including body, lenses, filters, and carrying case.

The sales promotion department had put together a neat package, including an illustrated catalog, to accompany the printed set of rules. There would be a wrap-up weekend at a centrally located resort hotel and a victory banquet during which the prize winners would be announced.

It sure sounded good when you presented the program to management. In fact, it still sounds good on paper. How come it didn't meet expectations? How come you went over the expense budget, spending almost 8% instead of the 6.5% overlay? How come bookings increased only 6% instead of the 17.5% you had promised?

You had planned the data quite thoroughly. You had what you thought was a commitment from the entire sales team. You look bad at the moment, but you will recover. Your marketing vice-president is a veteran of the "sales wars." He won't withdraw his support for you. But, he is asking you to explain what happened—why were the targets for expenses and for bookings missed? And, both of you want to know what lessons are to be learned that can be applied to future incentive programs—lessons that might help increase the success rate.

It seemed that everyone, staff and line people, was turned on by the whole thing. The promotion and advertising group did its thing and prepared a neat set of materials for distribution to each member of the sales force. Direct mail and space advertising programs went into action. You personally visited each of the field sales offices and, like a good coach, gave pep talks to everyone. "You guys and gals have done this before, producing outstanding results under great pressure! You can do it again. And, this time, there are extra rewards based on self-improvement in writing new orders. Go, team, GO!"

In retrospect, you now admit to yourself that you sensed something was not quite right. The responses, reactions, body language, and voices were not tingling with the kind of excitement you felt. You sensed that your people were listening to every word you were saying during these pep talks, but they didn't, you now admit to yourself, reflect your own excitement.

You should have paid attention to your instincts and the

weak and puzzling vibes you were getting. But, things had gone so far down the pathway that there was no turning back. Well, you might not have had to turn back. You just might have had to make some adjustments to the incentive program to strengthen its weak points. However, you are only human and, subconsciously, you repressed the negative signals you were getting from your sales team. They were tossing the ball to you, but you missed the throw. You blew it, coach!

There are several ways to handle this situation now. Yes, it is too late to fix the past quarter's results. However, there are ways to reduce the probability of a recurrence. Let's see if we have properly analyzed what happened. The effect is known, but what about cause and prevention? Once more, let's take the "options route" to definition, cause, and solution.

THESE ARE YOUR OPTIONS

A. Face-saving is important to you. The Orientals are always concerned about saving face, and they conduct themselves accordingly. And, from a management standpoint, they seem to do all right. You will profess total puzzlement about the quantitative failure of the sales promotion program. You will apologize to the marketing vice-president for not having made good on your commitment, and will then offset this with a review of your many successes. In good time, the whole thing will be forgotten.

B. You did your best; you planned well; you communicated thoroughly, in person and in writing. If anybody fell down on the whole thing, it was the field sales group. They did accept the 20% overlay in quota; you didn't force it on them. They are, in effect, in breach of contract with you. You will "lay it on them" quite solidly. You will tell your boss that you are totally disappointed in the aggregate performance of the sales group, just as he is. And, to make sure this doesn't happen again, you are making an immediate round of the field offices for private talks with each of the sales people. They are the ones who let you, the department, and the division down. They had better know this, and you will make sure they also know this is the last time such a thing will happen—as long as they work for you!

C. Strong, but contrite, is one way to describe your approach to management and to your field sales group— "strong" because this isn't the end of the world and "contrite" because the department as a whole, including you, fell down. On the positive side, total bookings did go over the original plan for the quarter. Expenses also went over the budget. However, the total impact can only be evaluated by the financial department and, as part of the whole, the over-budget dollars may be quite insignificant. You and everyone else can't ignore an over-budget situation. But, you will search for the lesson that is to be learned from this specific incident.

Why didn't you note—or did you note, but ignore it—the fact that your program was going over the budget? Was there a lack of real-time data? Were you given information on actuals versus budget too late to take action? Did your sales administrator collect information, maintain up-to-date records, analyze the facts and feed them back to you on a timely basis? Whatever the cause, you will make sure it doesn't happen again—by correcting what has to be your own falldown as a manager. Well, this may take care of the over-budget situation, as far as the future is concerned. You will discuss your findings, conclusions, and recommendations about monitoring and controlling future budgets with your boss. So much for responsiveness to management on budgetary matters. What about the falldown in bookings?

D. Well, Options A, B, and C did offer you a choice of actions. However, there is another possible route to follow. You will make the rounds of the field offices and have your private talks. However, the tone of the conversations with your people will not be accusatory. It will be inquisitive. You are searching for information and not seeking to identify culprits; this is not a guilt trip. There is a very important lesson to be learned by you, and you believe the teachers in this instance are your sales people. You will congratulate each one for having made an effort to make the program successful. In fact, in a mature and business-like way, you will show them the data concerning expenses and bookings and actuals versus plans. You will admit to each of the sales peeople that you had some uneasiness about the program from the very start. However, you ignored this uneasy sensation, hoping it would eventually all work out. You will ask them to discuss with you their initial reactions and their continuing feelings about the details of the program. What did they really think of the whole idea? You will listen closely and responsively, making certain not to squelch or argue with any of the points that are expressed. You are there to learn. Do you think you will learn?

DISCUSSION OF OPTIONS (PRO AND CON)

The human side of a materialistic program is one of the easiest to overlook, and probably the most frequently overlooked aspect of any incentive program intended to "inspire" sales people to new levels of achievement. Douglas McGregor, Professor of Psychology at MIT, leader in organizational behavior, and author of the classic book *The Human Side of Enterprise,** created the observations known as Theory X and Theory Y. While he did not describe management styles or write a manual on how to be a successful manager, McGregor postulated that there were two divergent viewpoints of human behavior in the work environment. Those who subscribe to Theory X believe that people do not want to work. They have to be disciplined severely. They work

* Douglas McGregor, *The Human Side of Enterprise* (New York: McGraw-Hill, 1960).

only for the material gains that work provides—the quantified pay and physical reward. Theory X proclaims that workers respond to the tough boss who carries a "stick"—and uses it when he sees the needs to do so. Those who subscribe to Theory Y believe that man needs to work in his search for material gain; but, they also believe man has strong emotional needs that he attempts to satisfy through his work. These needs are definable as several related but different factors, one of which is *recognition* as an individual.

In practice, those managers who subscribe to Theory X are among those who use such unpleasant clichés as "If you do your job, you get to keep it," and "A day's pay is what you get for a day's work." Or, such a manager might ask the question: "I pay you money. What else can you possibly want from me?"

Managers who identify with Theory Y intuitively believe that pay is essential for buying bread and shelter, and for providing physical comforts and security to the worker and his family. However, they also believe that "man does not live by bread alone;" there are other things, nonphysical and nonmaterial, that are of vital value to the worker. Workers do need a minimum number of dollars with which to satisfy the physical needs for bread and shelter. But, man can eat just so much bread and occupy just so much living space. When he has earned enough to satisfy these physical needs, money diminishes in importance. Other needs become his motivators. These include recognition as a superior individual.

Perhaps McGregor's observations offer a clue as to what went wrong—or what was overlooked in the development and implementation of the fourth-quarter sales-incentive program.

Consider the fact that your sales people earn incomes that, by any method of measurement of comparison, are quite reasonable and certainly above the national average for families. They can and do, without special promotion programs, provide very nicely for their own and their families' needs. Sure, the prizes were luxurious and nobody would turn one of them down. But, they were still only material things. If one of your people wanted any of the prizes for personal use, he probably could have gone out and bought it for cash or on credit.

So, what was missing here? Now it comes through. The need requiring satisfaction among your sales people is not necessarily the desire for material wealth. It is the need for recognition—the need to be held up and described among one's peers as being a special person, that is, a higher achiever than others. However, there was no provision anywhere in the plan to acknowledge and satisfy this need.

In the light of this, the options offered and which you have prepared on your own take on clear values. Let's review Options A though D (and those you developed) and determine (1) what was missing from the program, and (2) what we have learned and can apply to future incentive programs.

A.   An apology is in order; the expression of puzzlement without a statement of intent to define the cause is not. The review of your past successes is probably not necessary and can be interpreted as a defensive tactic which will not be appreciated. This option leaves the whole situation somewhere in limbo. It is unwise to think that the incident will be forgotten as time goes by. It will amaze you how well people remember our mistakes, and how forgetful they are of our successes.

B.   Rank has its uses, but this is not one of the most admirable. In this option you are using your rank entirely for power. You are passing the buck or "scapegoating." You have to recognize that, by now, everybody knows that the program was something less than successful and that you are in the frying pan. You will not succeed in putting them into your frying pan without getting severely burned yourself. *You blew it!* You won't succeed in convincing anyone, your sales people or your vice-president, that it was "the other guy's fault!" Don't try this one.

C.   Now you are moving in a constructive, lesson-learning direction. Remember that there were two problems in a single wrapper—over-budget and under-booking. You share in the failures as well as in the successes of your department. Next time, perhaps you will establish an improved results-reporting system of management information, one that will provide you with real-time data on budgets—actual versus plan—as well as on sales. This is not really an option. As sales manager, you are responsible and accountable for the control of both expenses and sales. There are no valid excuses for not having been aware of the fact that you were going over budget. There is no excuse for not reporting and discussing this fact with your own manager so that he could, at the very least, be spared a very unpleasant surprise. And, such a discussion would most likely have given him the opportunity to bring in the support you needed at the time to do the job properly. Next time, you will more adequately fulfill the role of fiscal as well as team manager. But this time, you blew it! A good lesson has been learned and you will make certain that everyone shares its benefits.

D.   As with Option C, you are continuing to move in a positive direction. You are now using rank properly—the rank you gained on the basis of your knowledge of sales and sales people. The sincerity of your search for answers will certainly bring out the best in your people. It is predictable that they will level with you on many matters, and they will take full advantage of the opportunity you offer in two-way communications as you exercise this option. Some of the "leveling" will be on matters not directly related to the contest. However, remember that you are on a fact-finding mission and truth-seeking venture. Listen and learn!

Among the things you will learn will be the answers to your question: "How did I blow it?" You will learn that the progress of the program should have been reported more frequently and quite differently to those involved. A periodic newsletter would have been appreciated. Such a bulletin could have been used to keep everyone, staff and line people, advised of the progress each of the sales people was making toward his goals. The writing style didn't have to be professional; but, perhaps someone in the advertising department or a free-lance writer could have done a good job of humoring and good-naturedly prodding the people in the field and the support people back at the office. The real value of this sort of communication is in the recognition it would give regularly to all the participants—"Hey, look, my name's in this newsletter!"

You could have taken it a big step further. Look at the way you "delivered" the car to the top winner. He had to go to the local dealer designated by the rules and hassle with him on how to get the car out of the shop, licensed, and documented. Next time, arrange for the division manager, your own boss, to personally escort the winner to the dealer and then drive him home in the new car. His family will thus share in the recognition the company has given him. A local photographer could also take pictures of the event for distribution to the local newspaper and to the company's promotion department for use in the employee newspaper. Use the same technique (select other managers or executives who can participate) with other major prizes that are too big to be hand-carried.

Those prizes that can be hand-carried can be awarded during the celebration or victory banquet. In addition, invite the spouses of the sales people to join you at the resort and at the banquet. The benefits in added recognition will far outweigh the costs.

Budget for these events in your next sales-boosting program. Obtain real-time information on income and outcome, and use this information to alert yourself as to whether or not the financial situation is under control. Manage the event as well as the people. Be aware that high achievers, and this may very well describe-your sales people, have needs that must be satisfied and that go well beyond material values.

Combine Options C and D in your next sales-incentive program. Too bad you blew this one. But, there will be a next time!

15 SNIPER

*An Ambush for
the Newest Member
of the Sales Team*

Trouble, again! Another one of your people has quit, left the job and the company. It's hard enough to find good people and harder to lose them. The boss is beginning to wonder about your ability to hold onto those who, after much searching and interviewing (all of which are expensive uses of time), don't stay on the job long enough for anyone to determine whether or not they were good, mediocre, or not worth keeping.

Your track record of keeping and motivating people, especially the top producers, has been excellent—until recently. You don't think you've changed your personality, style, or demands. But, nonetheless, something's gone haywire. There's trouble again, and you don't know the cause, much less the cure.

WHY, OH WHY, DO THEY LEAVE SO SOON?

You have been aware that the people who left the company and your department recently were emotionally distressed at the time they quit. There was no reason to believe they were other than very stable people when you and personnel interviewed them. None of them seemed particularly distressed, uneasy, or restless. Each had a good set of credentials. Reference checks never revealed any personality problems or emotional traumas, at least not while on the job. Each passed the interview cycle with top honors. Well, you certainly did not expect any unusual difficulties beyond the usual adjustment interval that always comes with new people who enter a new environment. Everyone makes allowances for time to "get acquainted." Sure, some require less time than others; but you and your boss have always practiced patience and allowed for a "learning curve" to fit the individual need.

Well, personnel and the boss are beginning to make oblique comments and not-so-funny remarks about how "you are slipping a bit, old boy!" Perhaps it's time to call for assistance; that is, do an "attitude survey" of the people who report to you. You could do such a survey yourself, asking your people to level with you and try to help you find the answer to the dilemma that, if no corrective action is taken, could seriously endanger your own position as a manager. While you may not be the cause of the problem, you "own" it now. You are certainly expected to identify the cause and recommend an appropriate cure.

Hold on for a moment. You could do the attitude survey yourself. But, how would you go about it? This is more in line with the skills of a specialist in organizational behavior, and deals with how people respond to their supervisors, peers, work, and the work environment. What's more, if you are the cause of the problem (the reason why people are leaving), how can you realistically expect your people to level with you to the extent of saying, "Hey, boss, wise up! It's you who's the problem!" Not too many people will demonstrate enough courage to tell the boss he's wrong, even if they honestly think he is. You never led any of your people to think it would be wise to be a "yes-man" while working for you. In fact, you think you've always had an open relationship with them. But, somehow this strikes you as being different. Everyone seems to avoid the subject of how short a time new people are staying with your operation, or how quickly they choose to leave. Are you being overly sensitive or are you reacting appropriately to the environment? What should you do? You may try one or more alternate paths. For example:

1. Call a meeting of the group; or, if you have periodic group meetings, make use of the time to let everyone know that you feel something is not quite right. Ask for comments. Be as nonthreatening as possible. Admit freely that you are puzzled and would welcome any thoughts on the subject that is causing you concern. Invite them to come to your office if they feel inhibited at the moment.

2. Invite your people into your office one at a time. Tell them of your concern. Solicit any thoughts that might shed some light on the situation.

3. Ask personnel to conduct an attitude survey that would not involve you as an interviewer of your people. It would be made clear during the interviews that no names would be identified—viewpoints, attitudes, and opinions would be disclosed anonymously. The facts are really all you want.

4. If personnel does not have the skill or staff (or if you do not have a personnel department) to prepare, conduct, and analyze such a study (it does require special preparation and experience), perhaps a consultant can be brought in to handle the entire affair on a free-lance basis.

Which course would be the one most likely to succeed? The answer lies in a determination of whether or not you and the company's personnel department can be totally objective and nonthreatening. Few of us can be totally objective, especially when we are so personally involved in the situation. This requires an objective person from outside, a third party with appropriate credentials and skills.

Let's move on to a later time period. The attitude survey has been completed and you are satisfied that the person responsible for collecting and analyzing the information has been quite objective during the entire process. At the very least, there is no indication that your people have been disturbed by the consultant's (or by personnel's) presence and the closed-door interviews.

You soon have the report and its conclusions. And, does it ever contain a surprise for you!

The finger does not point at you. But, it does point very clearly at the behavioral pattern of a member of your own staff, someone who has been with you for some length of time. In fact, this staff member has been with you longer than anyone else in your entire group. You had always recognized this person as being one of your most loyal people, overtly dedicated to you and to the company. It is hard to believe, but the facts are there, supported by virtually everyone in your group. It is especially interesting to note one of the comments made by the interviewer:

> Staff person C was the only one who claimed not to have noticed that many new hires were staying for only a short time. This person was a self-proclaimed loner.

How do you identify this specific person when the interviewees and their comments were supposed to be anonymous? Well, the pieces just fall into place.

Piece 1.   This person, now recognizable as C, came to your office every time you brought in a new hire to offer assistance in "breaking in" the new member of the group. It appeared to be a very nice offer each time. But, now you wonder whether or not C was trying to help or, in reality, trying to get inside information on what role the new hire was brought in to play within the group.

Piece 2.   C often came to your office with some bit of gossip about the new hire's habits or behavior. In retrospect, this information was not constructive or terribly positive, but more in the nature of a complaint or quite negative.

Piece 3.   C always asked you, with a probing manner that you sometimes found quite irritating, how this new hire was going to affect his own responsibilities or job assignment.

Piece 4.   C came excitedly to your office each time the new hire quit. The discussion, started by C, was always in the nature of an "I told you so—he wouldn't last very long in this company."

Piece 5.   You had been ignoring the fact that C was a loner. He rarely ever joined the others for lunch, a beer, or bowling. You credited C with a highly developed sense of competition and rationalized that the company was the beneficiary of this intense dedication to work.

You didn't and don't intend to breach the security and anonymity promised during the attitude survey. You won't break your word. However, note the commonality of the comments of the others in the group. Here are some examples:

EXAMPLE 1.   Every new hire, especially the ones who seemed to offer the promise of being effective, would find C (not identified by name in the final report) hovering, looking very closely and rudely over his shoulder.

EXAMPLE 2.   Every new hire would find C making very severe criticisms of his personality on the job.

EXAMPLE 3.   Every new hire would be the subject of a string of put-down comments from C.

EXAMPLE 4.   Every new hire would be the victim of continuous and cruel carping from C.

EXAMPLE 5.   Every new hire, even after having done a task well or having closed a tough sale, would receive a lecture from C about how he would have handled it.

EXAMPLE 6.   C rarely, if ever, had a kind word to say or ever gave any encouragement to the new hires during their break-in periods.

This is all very revealing, and according to the anonymous comments from the group, C has a nickname—*Sniper*. This characterizes the apparent fact that he is always sniping at the new hires, shooting them down, and turning them off just when they needed to be encouraged and turned on.

There is no doubt about it in anyone's mind. According to the survey, Sniper has been driving these new hires out of the company. The more promising the new hire, the stronger Sniper's efforts have been to get him out! This is distasteful to you, of course, but you accept the validity of the survey method. The analysis and the report seem so logical, despite the shocking and disenchanting revelations.

Now you have a dual dilemma. You don't really want to lose C. He's a high achiever as a sales person, he makes significant contributions to gross sales dollars, and you know your competitor across town would grab him (in fact, he has already made offers that you know about). That's one part of the dual dilemma—you can't fire C without hurting your sales. The other part is a question: "How can you modify Sniper's behavior from *destructive* to *constructive?*" You have several options available to you and you will present them, with your optimized choice, to your immediate supervisor.

THESE ARE YOUR OPTIONS

A.   Sniper—what a deplorable nickname to tack onto a person! However, C has earned this dishonorable monicker.

It takes some careful thought on your part to revise or reverse the behavior pattern that C has developed. You know C wasn't at all like this when he became part of your team some years back. You've probably changed somewhat yourself; you hope any changes have been for the better. You are aware of the difficulty of being objective, especially about one's own self. It helps, sometimes, to have someone whom you regard highly level with you—speak candidly and constructively about your personal behavior as seen through the eyes of your peers and superiors. You will give this sort of objective view directly to C. You will call him into your office for a "friendly" cup of coffee, close the door, and begin the discussion with a casual comment such as, "C, you and I have been together through a lot of rough times, and some good times too. We've always been straight with each other, calling it like we saw it, helping each other grow with the company." (This will conjure up visions of the good old days and soften what is about to come.) You continue: "I guess we have gone on doing our things here and, maybe, sometimes we lose sight of the objectives of our jobs."

C will probably loosen up a bit as he realizes the warmth of your espression. You will move rapidly and directly now to the reason why you have called him into your office. You will tell him about his nickname and the results of the attitude survey, which point to him as the direct cause for the premature departure of a number of the new hires. It is definitely not your style, you believe, to threaten or punish your subordinates for misbehavior. But, in this case, you feel it is important to advise C that you would appreciate his total cooperation in the future with every one of the new hires you bring into the group. You hope he will rid himself of the nickname Sniper as quickly as possible. In fact, you advise him that you intend to redo the attitude survey in about three months and you expect a completely different report on his behavior and peer relationships to show up by then. Also, you suggest it would be wise for him to participate more actively in social gatherings with his peers. "I will be watching for your improvement," you will conclude as you rise to signal that the meeting is over.

B.   You are not alone in this. You didn't create the nickname Sniper. Some of your subordinates did. They can't, much as they would like to, abdicate responsibility for C's behavior. You will call a staff meeting which everybody is required to attend. You will let them all know you are aware of a personality conflict within the group and that, instead of inventing clever nicknames, their time would be better spent in giving help to those who need help. Without referring to C, who is also in the meeting room, and without stating the specific results of the attitude survey, you will describe what you know of the artificial and painful environment that has been created and that has caused some people with great potential to quit their jobs. "This behavior has cost the company considerable time and money and has also caused me much embarrassment as a manager, and I want to see some changes made around here. Then the zinger—"Or, I'll make some changes myself that you might not like at all!"

C.   Another possibility is that you will call your subordinates into your office one or two at a time, so as not to be conspicuous about this delicate matter. Over a cup of coffee, you will let them know you are aware of the personality problem with C and how it has literally driven some high-potential people out of the company. You will ask them to become personally and constructively involved in helping C to change. You will suggest they make a special effort to be more friendly with him, and perhaps include him in some of their social activities. Anything they can do to help the situation will be appreciated. You feel certain they will come through for you. The benefits to everyone and to the company are obvious.

D.   "Nobody is perfect." An old cliché, but how important it is to recognize its validity at this moment. While it is true that your job description never included the authority to play the role of some sort of super being or even that of a minor divinity, there is no doubt now that the role of the manager includes the ability to perceive the needs of his subordinates. Through this perceptive ability he is expected to enable his subordinates to satisfy those needs that are directly related to job performance. Fundamentally, this is what motivation and productivity are all about. So, Sniper is not perfect, and, because you took him for granted, you are also not perfect. Perhaps this is the time for some introspection and self-examination. You've seen Sniper's effect; now you must find the cause of this undesirable behavior and develop a cure.

There are several possible explanations for Sniper's extraordinary behavior and each deserves investigation. You will ask him to join you in your office for some "one-on-one brainstorming." He will probably be flattered by the invitation and accept readily. "This is not a command performance," you will say to C. "I have a problem and want to talk it over with you, gain the benefit of our joint thinking." Brainstorming is a problem-solving technique that, when properly implemented, works quite effectively.

You won't play cat-and-mouse with C. You will, without hostility or haste (you will choose a time for the meeting when you are not feeling any anger), point out that you have been known to make mistakes and that you learned valuable lessons from most of them. However, this one is a bit different from the others in that it involves C and a certain behavior pattern. You will point out that you see one of your responsibilities as providing guidance and direction to your people, and you would now like to do this for C.

C will probably listen with some nervousness, anticipating that he is about to be told off, criticized, and be read a "riot act." You will not prolong this moment of unpleasantness. You will tell him how concerned you are about the high turnover rate among the new hires. You will tell him you feel badly that he has not taken a stronger role in breaking in and helping them get off to a good start.

In all likelihood, C will be genuinely surprised to hear that he hasn't been "helping." He might even infer that you are saying he has done the opposite. But, you will deliberately avoid labelling his behavior as being "bad," "negative," or "damaging." You will now become more specific, listing some of the "do's" you would like to see everyone in the department practice with respect to new hires.

Do   be hasty with positive criticism. The guy may be doing his best, and his best will improve with time and experience on the job. Suppress the impulse to start a comment with a negative expression.

Do   stand behind the new guy and look over his shoulder while he does his paperwork, provided you have been invited to so so or have directly asked for permission to do so. Don't ever do this without permission. It makes one terribly nervous and highly self-conscious.

Do   listen to his telephone conversations, but only after you have first expressed your desire and willingness to offer a constructive critique and you have been invited to do so.

Do   state every one of your critiques in a positive manner; avoid negative statements. Express all comments in a constructive and complimentary way. It can't be all bad. Accentuate the good aspects of the work being done by the new person.

Do   build up the ego. Every person who is new on a job feels some uncertainty and insecurity.

The start-up period in a new job is like the formative years of a child. Success or failure can be linked with the environment into which one has been thrust. Be extra careful to avoid any put-downs.

Do   let me (the manager) hear from you directly about the new hire's growth, as well as his problem or difficulties as you view them. But, don't forget or omit the positive comments when you report the negative ones.

Do recognize that I (the manager) need, want, and welcome your assistance in building a strong sales force. Often, we have to grow our own from inexperienced "seedlings." Remember that once upon a time we were seedlings ourselves.

Do be on your own guard against the tendency we may have to put others down when we really should be building them up.

You will suggest periodic meetings with C in which he and you will discuss the merits and demerits of the new hires or trainees that are brought into the group. Together, you and he will help them become models he can point to with pride as "his product." You will explain that you and he will be helping each other overcome some of your own imperfections in getting along with other people. Both of you could eventually become role models for the group to emulate. These are the things you will discuss with C on an ongoing basis.

DISCUSSION OF OPTIONS (PRO AND CON)

The responsibility for doing work belongs to the subordinates in an organization. The sales manager is accountable for the completion of the tasks and for meeting objectives established for the group and for himself—such as meeting quotas, monitoring and controlling expenses, and building the organization and its individual members through training and motivation. Ideally, the successful sales manager is both effective and popular. Sometimes, a choice has to made between one and the other. One may achieve popularity among his subordinates by being just "one heck of a nice guy." Excellent, if this state can be achieved while being effective and popular with one's superiors. It is difficult to imagine a vital decision being made concerning a sales manager's future on the basis of the argument that says, "Mr. Manager may not meet his quota (again), but look how well-liked he is!"

Each of us who works in a formalized business structure is simultaneously a subordinate and a superior within the hierarchy of the total organization. We are superior to our subordinates, and subordinate to our superiors. However, this means that in our roles as superiors we are accountable for the work performed by our subordinates. At the same time, we are responsible to our own superiors for the aggregate productivity or output of our subordinates. At first reading, this may sound like an exercise in semantics. But, if you will reread and evaluate the thought, you may find a clue to some of the reasons why many of our subordinate managers (region, district, zone, or area) can become confused. It can be difficult to separate those things for which one is *accountable* from those for which we are *responsible.*

One way to avoid such a dilemma is to abdicate responsibility and adopt a *laissez-faire* (leave-alone or do-nothing) style of management. Let the chips fall where they may—it will all work itself out in the long run, won't it? Leave them alone and they'll come home. Will they?

It would appear that what happened here was a situation in which the manager lost contact with his people. He sensed yet he ignored the signs of trouble. He abdicated his responsibility. In all likelihood, he finally took action when an alarm signal was transmitted to him by his boss. And, when he tried to take action, he was lost. He knew neither the cause nor the cure. In fact, he had a difficult time defining the problem. He did, however, demonstrate wisdom and courage by calling for help from other resources. He ultimately gained a definition of the specific problem, its likely cause, and most probable remedy.

But, beware! His judgment might be faulty. He might panic. He might even make things worse. In fact, some of the options being considered could make things much worse than they already are. Once again, you are the sales manager in this hypothetical situation. Let's examine the options that were proposed and determine which holds the greatest promise for success.

A.   This starts out as the "fatherly" approach—the nurturing parent who offers solace and consolement. At best, it is insincere and will probably be recognized as some sort of come-on. At worst, it will evoke a response such as, "Who does he think he is, talking to me like some brat; he's not my daddy!" It's not your style to threaten. This approach has many inferred threats built on a set of orders to C to change his way of doing things. The implication is that you've seen the results of the attitude survey and anything that's gone wrong is C's fault. You can't order or command him to become more sociable. And your final shot, as you signal the end of the meeting, will probably come across as an ultimatum with a threat of the most dire of consequences. Even though it is not your intent, C would quite likely update his resumé and start looking for another job.

B.   If this is your preferred option, you are denying any responsibility (even though you have accountability) for the events that led to Sniper's development. Remember, he was not this way when he first joined your group. While some of Sniper's character aberrations might have been caused by personal problems, outside the company and beyond your control or influence, you are still accountable for his behavior during business hours.

This comes across as a "pass-the-buck" situation. You are laying it all at the feet of your subordinates with a threat of "change things, or else!" What's more, you broke the confidentiality of the attitude surveys. Those who revealed their feelings and the nickname Sniper to the interviewer will feel betrayed, as well as wrongly accused of guilt and of being a cause of this situation. Your next attitude survey will probably produce very inaccurate information and few facts. People will be reluctant to reveal their observations next time.

C.   This is certainly preferrable to Options A and B in

that you are not abdicating responsibility for the situation. Then, again, you aren't exactly accepting responsibility either. It sounds more like you are neatly passing the buck to the rest of the team. The difference between Options B and C is that the "or else" threat is omitted. What do you do for an encore if this one doesn't work out? As with Option B, you may have blown the "cover" off the attitude survey.

D.   You've made a very important admission to yourself: It is entirely possible that some of the fault lies with you. You apparently had a lot of confidence in C and left him pretty much to his own devices. However, remember that not many subordinates enjoy being left to their own devices. Many need and want recognition and attention from the boss. Some will go to strange, exaggerated, and dangerous lengths to get it.

In this situation, you perceive that C has been seriously starved for attention. He is not able, as a person, to be a socializer. He is dedicated to his work and his job. you never denied this, and always recognized that he was a high achiever. Perhaps you didn't recognize how dedicated he was to you as his boss. He sought, and did not receive, adequate attention. Some of us have a greater need than others for attention, recognition, applause, or praise for a good performance on a regular basis. What harm would there have been in letting C and the rest of the group know how highly you regard his performance? In fact, a great deal of good would have come from such a action on your part toward each individual performing well. Adults as well as children want to know where they stand. Both may behave undesirably or erratically when denied this knowledge. Through your silence, C felt denied. Option D can restore your channel of communication with him and restore his self-esteem, which depends so much on you for "feeding."

Through Option D, you have not breached the security of the attitude survey which has been so helpful to you. The problem's cause and cure have been identified. At no time in your conversation have you revealed your knowledge of the deplorable nickname of Sniper. You haven't attached a label to C's behavior. You have followed a logical path to a workable solution to the problem. C's need has been recognized and you have taken action to avoid recurrences of "need-starvation." You and C have developed a new "contract," restoring your fine relationship. Probably, C will feel a new sense of motivation and both of you may even discover that, from the standpoint of maximum capability, he has been an underachiever.

What about you, personally? Your own self-esteem and the respect you deserve from your subordinates, peers, and superiors have been significantly enhanced. You can hardly wait for that new fellow you hired to show up for work! He'll never know about the past, but he will have a bright experience in an inspiring environment.

No doubt about it, Option D is the winner!

16 LOCUS-INCOGNITUS

Where, Oh Where,
Has This Sales Man Gone?

"Where is he now?" That's the question you have been asking. "Where is he now?" Everyone, in fact, has been asking that one. But, this particular sales man's whereabouts are usually unknown. Most of the time he is *Locus-Incognitus*, at some location that is not known to you or to others in your group.

Speaking of loners, this fellow behaves as though he doesn't have a care in the world for rules and regulations and, for that matter, doesn't seem to care whether or not you know it. Part of the problem is that he is out in the "boon-docks," in a territory that is hardly considered "choice pickings" but that must be covered nevertheless. Despite the jokes and tittering about being in the middle of nowhere, the territory has been making a contribution to profitability. Relatively speaking, taking territorial limitations into account, your man, generally referred to as Locus-Incognitus—whereabouts unknown—is productive.

167

KNOWING WHERE, AND WHEN, AND WHAT

So what's the gripe? It's a typical manager's gripe—you are accountable for his comings and goings and for territory coverage and management which is an integral element in the productive application of selling time, but you rarely know where this sales person is at any given moment. More than just embarrassing, you are not sure whether the guy is really working for you and the company, or for himself and who knows what else. This has to cease!

Oh, you've tried the usual procedures of reminding him of the requirement to file advance itineraries and to check in with the office at least once a day. You've reminded him of the requirement to file call reports at the end of each week of travel. But he goes his own way, merrily or otherwise. You just don't know the reasons for his lack of proper response to your instructions. It is time you did something about it— something that won't turn him off, but that will make him recognize that he is part of a group (a carefully developed team with no room for rebels and loners). As the manager, you are accountable for him.

Doesn't he remind you of other situations you've had to deal with before? There's a touch of Seat-of-His-Pants, the fellow who refused to plan ahead. He reminds you of Stiff-Fingers, who wouldn't get reports to you on a timely basis. However, this one adds a new variable—he goes "on the road" without giving you notice, and he returns to the office on his own private schedule.

Locus-Incognitus is quite popular with the rest of the group. In fact, you are rather fond of him yourself. He has a very likeable and disarming personality, always offering positive words and displaying an unflappable sense of humor. It's nice to be around a guy like this. To use an overused phrase, "he is well-liked." However, you know there is a big difference between being *well-liked* and being *respected*. One can be well-liked just because of a sunny disposition—

which will beat the grouchy type in any popularity contest. It is, in the business world at least, more preferable to be respected as a person with high integrity, honesty, knowledge, and dependability. With this respect, generally speaking, comes a highly desirable kind of popularity.

It is said that it is difficult to be both popular and effective. Yet, many of your peers and your superiors at the top of the organization chart are doing it. Their popularity is born out of the respect or the high esteem in which they are held. They are good role models for your own behavior and growth.

Well, back to the problem at hand. It is coming to a head because you have been embarrassed too many times by your lack of knowledge of the territory covered by Locus-Incognitus. He doesn't report his road plans and rarely sends in all reports. Lost-sale reports, so valuable to you in developing sales strategies in order to cope more effectively with competition, just don't come from him. Nobody's perfect! So, he must be losing some sales and it is vital to know what the opportunities are in the territory. His sales record has been consistently good. But, now you are beginning to wonder whether or not it could be better. You are becoming increasingly aware of your own lack of knowledge of his particular territory and the accounts. Are they growing or are they shrinking in potential? The record shows they are static in units purchased. The dollars have been going up entirely because of inflation and price increases. What is happening to your share of the market? Is it up, down, or unchanged? There are many unanswered questions here, and you are now determined to get the answers.

There are many ways you can go about resolving this puzzler. Too often we jump at the first idea that comes to mind. By this time, however, you have learned that there are usually several options open to you and, although most of them will work, one is invariably best—for the long term. It's time to line up your options, evaluate each one as objectively as you can, discuss them with your superior, gain his support for the option in which you have the greatest confidence, and then take action.

THESE ARE YOUR OPTIONS

A.   You are very much aware of your man's popularity and, therefore, will proceed with caution. You certainly do not want anyone to get the impression that you are singling him out for a close-inspection drill. (Even though you are singling him out from the rest of the group, you want to be as subtle and as inoffensive as possible about it.) You will call him on the phone—no, not to remind him to send in itinerary, call, and lost-sales reports. This request hasn't worked at all in the past.) This time, you will tell him you want to see him in your office on a very specific date and time. Naturally, he will want to know the reason for the summons. In fact, he might even protest that you are taking him out of the field just when he has some very "hot prospects" lined up. You will tell him, in such an event, that the visit will take no more than one or two days and it is important to you, and to him, that the two of you have a discussion about the territory.

You will insist and he will come. When he arrives, you and he will get right down to business. He will hear some direct and straight talk from you. You never were one to beat around the bush and you won't start doing so now. Get straight to the point and tell him that, henceforth, he will not leave the office (his field office) without filing an itinerary plan with you. No plan, no travel! And, within three days of his return, you expect a written report, just like the reports everyone else submits including details about who he called on, where the call was made, what was discussed, what interests were indicated by the prospect and, if there is a possibility for a sale to this account somewhere down the line, you want an estimate of probability (in the range of X% to Y%) for closing the sale and a time frame for doing it. Everyone else does this as a routine part of the selling job. You see no reason for exempting him from this requirement.

To make it all the more binding, you will hold back on his bonuses, commissions, and delay his performance appraisal (salary review) until you are convinced he is doing the "whole" job of selling on your team. You will also give him a time limit, say 90 days, to get his act together.

B.   There's a shortcut you might take. You will apply peer pressure! He is popular with his peers, indicating the probability that he wants to please them. So, you will get in touch with each one of his associates, tell them about the problem, and ask them to do what they can—for his sake—to get him to fall into line with your policies and procedures. It sounds painless, doesn't it?

C.   At the next sales meeting, you will have a major discussion with the group concerning the need for such details as are the root of the trouble you are having with Locus-Incognitus. Naturally, you won't mention any names. Those who are guilty, however, will get the message. Then, if the problem persists, Locus-Incognitus, and anyone else who chooses to ignore your regulations, will be openly and deliberately guilty of insubordination.

D.   You haven't visited Locus-Incognitus in the field; that is, you haven't had a "sidewalk critique" with him in quite some time. By now you perhaps owe him some of your time. So, you will plan such a visit, meeting with him first in his office for a strategy session prior to traveling the territory together. This will "kick off" with a telephone conversation in which you will tell him of your desire to travel with him for a while, say a week. Ask him to prepare an itinerary for both of you. It should list the accounts by name, location, and time that you and he will call on them; means of travel (plane or car); and the names and phone numbers of the hotels and motels you will be staying at—so you can be conveniently reached by your office, if necessary. (You wish he would learn to emulate your behavior in this matter.)

The week together will give you an excellent opportunity to have a number of talks with Locus-Incognitus concerning his time and territory management, and the reasons why you must have detailed information prior to and immediately following his travels. You never were one for remote-control or absentee management. Getting out into the field is important, specifically in connection with this particular situation. You expect to establish a new relationship with your man and, as a result, both of you will benefit.

DISCUSSION OF OPTIONS (PRO AND CON)

What do you suppose might be among the root causes for the behavior of Locus-Incognitus? There are several possibilities that we can think of. For example, this might be a way to get attention. Childish, perhaps, but quite possibly true. You admit you haven't paid much attention to him because of his boondocks location. He might be feeling a sort of second-class membership in the group.

It is also possible that he is just plain rebellious against symbols of authority. Rules and regulations, and you, are all symbols as well as actualities. This is again childish, and represents an unwillingness to accept adult on-the-job responsibility.

Also, he might not feel sure of himself. By being far away and hard to locate, he thinks he can keep you off his back. Have you been on his back very much? Do you nag him for sales? Do you praise him when he does well, even if he's doing just what is expected of him? The cliché holds that for every kick in the pants a sales manager gives to his people he should give two pats on the head. Well, the ratio of kicks to pats may be a variable, but, do you remember to provide the warm pats as well as the cold kicks? For some managers, it seems to be quite easy to kick, but difficult to pat. One is good for the recipient's self-esteem; the other can be destructive.

Well, we did recognize you are not a remote-control or absentee-type manager. It is time to put a stop to the guess-work and start collecting facts, to replace conjecture and opinion with data. Let's examine the probable effects of the various options presented previously.

A.   This is loaded with threats! The telephone call will no doubt create the impression that he is being "called on the carpet!" This is a command, and you give him no alternatives but to obey. All past efforts to make him follow the reporting requirements have failed. The threats or warnings that you will withhold his paycheck—which he has earned according to the same set of rules and regulations—could be illegal as well as ethically and morally undesirable. The time limit you set is a notice to him to start looking for another job. He might not be around for the first 90-day review target. This only makes matters worse for everyone concerned.

B.   This is most certainly a shortcut. But, it is a shortcut to advising your group that Locus-Incognitus has you on the run, that you are unable to manage him, and that you are admitting a weakness. You are abdicating your own role as manager, transferring it to your subordinates. Unlike delegating authority, a vital element in good management, this is abdicating authority. Have you ever noticed that not everyone wants to be a manager? With this option, you are delegating an important part of your managerial responsibilities to people who will, most likely, reject them.

C.   More threats and weakness, merely disguised as guidance and instruction. While it is always prudent to review the reporting requirements with the group, it may not be prudent to mention the dire results one can expect if the requirements are not fulfilled. And, while Locus-Incognitus may receive the message you are transmitting, it may come through distorted, therefore failing to achieve the desired result. This is too oblique.

D.   Obviously, this is the approach with the best chance for success. Time in the field with Locus-Incognitus is long overdue. It will enable you to collect facts and data that will lead you to a logical solution to the problem. If he is in need of recognition, this will provide it—on condition, of course, that you avoid verbal and nonverbal expressions of hostility while you are with him. By giving him advance notice of your visit, and by instructing him to preplan the trip and to let you know the schedule and other facts about the itinerary (which, not so incidentally, you are allowing him to establish), you are giving him an important demonstration of "how to" manage his territory and his time.

This is a positive approach. It should provide a valuable learning experience with high retention. While you are in the field, you will take time each day, in his presence, to telephone your office for messages. You will also suggest that he do the same thing. The telephone calls will be brief and to the point—no hassle and no threats for anyone. Each time you call you will reconfirm the next day's travel schedule with your office—and suggest he do the same thing.

At some time, perhaps during or after dinner, you will again describe the reasons for maintaining continuous contact and communications with the office. It's not because you feel it is necessary to constantly look over his shoulder. It is because he is an important part of the whole activity. The company, the group, and you need his part of the information so the whole "puzzle" of marketing and selling can be put together successfully.

You and he will both benefit from the face-to-face contacts with the accounts in the territory. You will be able to give him the so-called "sidewalk critiques" that, when constructively given, all professional sales people find quite valuable. These critiques will be especially appreciated when they come from someone he respects. They also provide a highly enhanced form of recognition.

Yes, this takes more work on your part than a telephone

call does. However, it is time for you to go out into the boondocks. You'd probably be more disturbed if his whereabouts were always inside the office instead of out there where the action is. This is the route to take and the option most likely to succeed.

17 MAÑANA

Don't Do Today
What You Can Put
Off Until Tomorrow

This hurts! You've managed your way through many problems that concerned people, products, services, and the unhappiest of customers. You are a professional sales man, a seasoned (meaning "well-formed") manager of people. Recruiting, training, developing, and enhancing the skills of people is one of your strengths. By now you believe you've seen it all. You've interviewed new candidates for positions with your company, more specifically with your department or section, for quite some time. You know that even the most professional personnel managers and career recruiters have not always made the best recommendations. But, you take pride in your own record of selection that has proven that you are right many more times than you are wrong. You had high hopes for this one. He's your administrator—or so you thought.

DEPENDING ON THE UNDEPENDABLE

Administrator, indeed! The person filling this job function should be among the, if not the most, dependable of people on your staff. However, much to your dismay, he isn't; he might even win the award for being the least dependable of all! He has the credentials for the position: an M.B.A. with a major in finance and several years of productive field sales experience. He appears to have an intelligence that shines and an ability to articulate ideas that holds any listener's undivided attention. He does display, though not consistently, reasonably good powers of communication. What is he doing in administrative work—an inside position? Why did he leave the career of selling out in the field? You had carefully checked his references before making him the job offer. When he stated that he was number 1 or 2 in sales in his last field-sales spot, he was not boasting one bit. It was the truth. Why did he leave? For very valid and very personal reasons, he could not be away from home or out of town for the length of time required to adequately cover a sales territory. The details are not important. Suffice it to say that his career is now in sales support, essentially a desk job. He wants to stay close to sales people, perhaps to share, vicariously, the excitement of "being out there where the action is!"

You liked the idea of having a top staff man who feels, understands, and likes the excitement of the "sale." He would require a minimum amount of training. And, best of all, he would be very sympathetic and empathetic as far as the idiosyncracies and demands of sales people go. These are managerial characteristics that are quite essential to creating, assembling, building, guiding, directing, monitoring, and controlling an effective sales team. You had high hopes—predominant among which were dependability; meeting deadlines; and having your data assembled, partially analyzed, and in your hands exactly when you needed it. Disenchantment of disenchantments! His deadline for completion of any task is dependably, as they say out West, *mañana!* He is never on time, never meets deadlines, and never hits a target date for completion. "Never" may be putting it a bit strongly. "Hardly ever" is, on the other hand, an accurate way to describe his work habits. "Tomorrow boss, for sure." Hence his nickname—*Mañana.*

What is the matter? He puts in long hours on the job. (You almost said "he works long hours," but you are not entirely sure "works" is the right verb). He arrives early and leaves late. He takes few coffee breaks and never a lunch break. He is apparently dilligent. He rarely visits with others in the office and frequently works with his door closed. You know what they say about those who tend to drop by for a chat: "The person who has time to kill usually kills yours." You had assumed that he closed his door so he could concentrate totally on his tasks. Now, because of his relatively low efficiency in terms of meeting target dates, you wonder about the accuracy of your assumptions.

The work he produces is almost excellent, and would be totally excellent if he would give you realistic commitment dates for completion and delivery. If your assumptions have been accurate and he is truly diligent and dedicated to his assigned tasks, just what is his problem? What's wrong with Mañana? Or, is something wrong with the way you manage him?

You have neither the time nor the desire to engage in a detailed analysis of Mañana's personal habits. You want to turn things around and find the formula that will result in changing your administrator from a *mañana* person into a *now* person. In fact, you have no other choice but to achieve a turnaround. And you can do it, provided you accurately evaluate the situation, list the courses of action you might take, and activate the best one. Let's give it a try. Your own thinking may be enhanced by the suggested options which follow.

THESE ARE YOUR OPTIONS

A.   Talk with him, man to man and friend to friend. Tell him about your distress concerning his apparent inability to keep his time commitments, usually deadlines he has set himself. You will try not to hurt his feelings, although you believe this is almost always impossible to do when you are criticizing a person's behavior. It is not your intent to hurt, but only to get to the root of this problem. Listen closely and responsively, just as you have learned to do in dealing with other situations wherein you were collecting facts. This will help in your effort to draw him out. If he acts surprised, and he might very well be surprised to hear your comments, you will firmly and politely let him know that "This is the way I see it!" Sometimes, there is an advantage in a surprise approach to a situation; you believe it brings out the truth that underlies the superficial and obvious. You will then "play it by ear" and, if he responds positively with a statement of intent to correct his behavior, tell him you will be watching him for signs of significant improvement. And, you *will* follow through by observing him carefully.

B.   Flexibility of style is a positive characteristic in a manager's behavior. He has to know when to "pull rank" and when to "lay back." He must be capable of a *laissez-faire* style in which he leaves everyone to his own devices for an appropriate time period. Then, he must be able to switch to the other extreme, becoming the authoritarian leader who gives tight direction and, if necessary, sets the pace for his troops by marching vigorously out in front (sort of a shirt sleeves approach; that is, showing the others by creating a model). It is possible that this is one of the times for the authoritarian mode. This time, when you talk to him about the problem, you will bring out a series of documents that have been logged with respect to the amount of time he has taken to complete each task.

You will give him a neatly detailed explanation of why, as you see things, it took him so long to do each of the tasks.

And, best of all, you will cap the discussion with a description of exactly how you would have approached and handled each of the assignments you had given to him. Thus, you are setting an example on how you analyze an assignment and race to the finish line—ahead of time, at best; on time, at least. Give him some ideas and guidelines on how to do it. Keep the discussion informal and friendly. Sometimes, informality, especially when it comes from the boss, is more effective than an exchange of memos. There, now you have given him the benefit of your experience in how to get things done. Watch him grow!

C.   On the other hand, nobody's perfect—including you. Admit it to yourself. You made a poor choice. Send him a short memo, with a copy to the personnel files, stating quite simply that you are dissatisfied with his work and you hope for an improvement within the next 45 days. Advise him that you are not firing him, but merely giving him a specific time period in which to learn to do those things that are expected. In 45 days, you will review his performance with him. He'll get the message; and if he really wants the job, he will make a sincere effort to improve.

D.   The thought occurs to you that he is relatively new at a desk job. He is more used to field sales and, perhaps, a less regimented and less visible routine. While effective selling does require careful planning and implementation, and does involve meeting deadlines, the field sales person usually has greater latitude in scheduling and controlling his time and deadlines. It is entirely conceivable that he simply doesn't know how to manage his time in this new administrative position. Did you take time to teach him those things you had learned when you made the move from outside line sales to inside staff? Probably not; you expected he would learn through on-the-job training. There is nothing basically wrong with this approach. Few people come to a new position all polished and up to speed from the first day. Some take longer than others, of course. Those that take longer may do so because of lack of guidance and direction rather than because of some inappropriately assumed lack of desire, motivation, or skills. If the elements of desire and motivation are present, the skills can be acquired. If the skills are present, they can be sharpened and improved through clearly defined guidance and direction. This is one of the options open to you. Take him in hand and show him the way. But how will you do this? We'll get right down to cases—options, that is.

DISCUSSION OF OPTIONS (PRO AND CON)

A.   If Mañana is made of stone and is devoid of any feelings of self-esteem, this might just work. The basis is that any comment, negative as well as positive, is accepted; not necessarily acted upon, but accepted in the sense of being received and heard. It is quite difficult, and often damaging to the ego, to be called into the boss's office for what amounts to a "chewing out" or a "talking to." He may be surprised to learn that he is not doing as well as you would like him to do. If he does appear to be genuinely surprised at your critique, then you have been remiss in your communications and appraisals. Some of the blame, or fault, is on your head. Using a surprise tactic in an effort to bring out the underlying truth is gamesmanship that should not be activated. Your rank will prevail. You will "win" the discussion. Your man will "lose" it. Knowing that you are looking over his shoulder or observing him will hardly motivate him to do more than look for other opportunities inside or outside the company.

B.   Yes, flexibility of style is important and all effecive managers learn how to be flexible. More important, they learn when to exercise flexibility. The style must be appropriate to the situation in order to be effective. In this option, you almost make it to a successful resolution. It's good to be specific, but bad to deal in generalities. You have your specifics—the facts all neatly assembled and documented. It sounds somewhat like a judicial hearing, however, rather than a discussion whose objective is to correct or resolve a difficulty. Your informality is commendable. But, it may miss its mark because it goes nowhere. This is a one-on-one seminar, a lecture that will probably leave you feeling less than satisfied and your man quite mystified. Although it is attempted quite often by managers, this option doesn't quite make the grade.

C.   This is a long way to a shortcut. You have given him 45 days to update his resume, complain to personnel, become unhappy, and leave the company. Guidance and direction, elements that may have been missing and which may be the fundamental problem, are quite absent from this option. He may sincerely want the job. However, the assumption that a 45-day review will cause him to improve his performance may be a very inaccurate assumption. The only thing this accomplishes is the avoidance of the restriction imposed upon you by the rules of this book that preclude firing a person as a way to resolve a situation. Good gamesmanship is evident in this option, but not good management.

D.   Too often, a person is brought into a new job situation on the basis of outstanding performance in a previous one. Certainly you've heard a veteran sales or marketing manager comment sadly, "I've taken many good sales men out of the field and made lousy desk managers out of them!" Tops in the field; awful in the office! This doesn't have to be way, provided you get off to the right start. And, if you didn't get off to the right start there may still be time to turn things around and get on the right track.

What is the problem here, basically? Mañana seems to be a bit lost; he's mystified by the process of establishing realistic objectives. He appears unable to steer himself in such a way as to assure that he will meet the targets. You are the person to show him how to do it. Call it "management by objectives," "results-oriented time management," or "self-discipline"—or call it by any set of buzz words that satisfy semantic needs. The vital thing is that Mañana needs help. You are well equipped to provide help in the form of specific guidance and instruction. You will do it in a logical fashion, much in the same way effective and pragmatic managers and planners do it when they have to implement and control complex, multifaceted activities. They use diagrams or flow charts of activities that define the individual steps that are essential to the completion of tasks. In this situation, you will use a specific example; that is, a task about to be started or one that has recently been set in motion.

The method is quite simple, concise, and explicit. The most valuable aspect of this approach to task-management is that it creates the effect of a "contract" between you and Mañana. A road map is formulated that shows the starting and ending points for the task with respect to time. All of the "stops" along the way become benchmarks for checking progress, again with respect to time and task. Any delays are immediately highlighted as danger signals. The signals enable corrective actions to be planned and implemented. The end-objective can be reevaluated at each mark to ensure that it continues to be realistic. Or, if the original map has become outmoded through changes in master plans, objectives, or any other reason, it can be redrawn or discarded, as necessary.

This "map," as we call the documented plan, is created while you and Mañana are together. It is a joint effort to assure agreement and mutual ownership and commitment. The document rarely needs to be more than one page long. Place a standard size sheet of note paper on its long edge. At the right edge of the sheet, draw a vertical line that reaches from the top to the bottom of the page. On this line, half way up from the bottom, draw a small square. Inside this square, write the date that represents the scheduled completion of the task. At the left edge of the sheet, draw another straight line that reaches from the top to the bottom of the page. Put the starting date for the task at the base of this vertical line.

Across the bottom of the sheet, draw a horizontal line that reaches from the vertical line at the left to the vertical line at the right. At various points along this horizontal line draw a series of small arrows. Position and label each arrow so as to indicate time intervals (days, weeks, or months; whatever calibrations are appropriate to the total time scale for the task). Then, draw a heavy line horizontally from the "completion square" at the right to the vertical line at the left. This straight line (the shortest distance between two points) indicates the "road" to follow to reach completion from the starting point.

You will review with Mañana the key steps or critical elements along the road to completion. When any one element of the total task is due to be started, draw a triangle resting on the horizontal "heavy line" at the center of the page at a point that is directly above the appropriate spot in reference to the time-line at the bottom of the page. Put a key letter or number inside the triangle and add a footnote that defines the meaning of the triangle.

When all key or critical points have been identified, entered, and labelled, you and Mañana will agree that the triangles are vital benchmarks. Whenever there is an indication that the due date of any one of the benchmarks is in jeopardy, Mañana will immediately bring the sheet, an explanation of the problem, and a proposed solution to you. Together, you will evaluate the potential impact on the objective and determine whether or not the project's plan or targets should be recalculated. Together, you will discuss your options, selecting, examining and agreeing upon the one that offers the greatest probability for success. You will then implement the appropriate actions. At the same time, you will establish target dates and benchmarks for reviews of the tasks and the progress being made.

Both of you now own the project. You are mutually committed and motivated to its success. Bet you make it! This option is the way to make it.

18 ROUNDUP TIME

*A Potpourri of
Problems and Solutions*

Not all situations encountered by a sales man, sales manager, or a sales department are matters of life and death. There are many situations that tend to bedevil a manager and cause some distraction from the primary task of prospecting and closing orders. They, for the most part, do not usually require deep thought or special approval and support from the manager's superiors. These situations are "run-of-the-mill" headaches. They are not superficial in their effects, yet not deep enough to require major surgery. The options are generally self-evident. "But," you say, "if they are 'self-evident' why can't I find a satisfactory solution?" Well, maybe its a case of being too close to the forest to see the trees. So, this chapter is dedicated to a series of run-of-the-mill problems and likely solutions.

Put your pad away. You won't have to be terribly creative as you read this chapter. In fact, you may even say to yourself as you read along "Heck, I know this one!" Fine, if you are familiar with a particular situation, you have most likely handled it appropriately before. However, many managers of people often overlook the obvious and search for deeper meanings in people-behavior than actually exists.

In this chapter we'll drop the nicknames and discuss some ways to cope with an interesting variety of sales people, those who always arrive late at sales meetings, are continuously in conflict with certain customers, oversell the customer on the merits of the product or service, provide useful management information that may be unintentionally hidden in their expense reports, confuse commands with reports, and consider a brainstorming meeting a place where people are supposed to exercise their egos and have powerful arguments.

NEVER ON TIME FOR THE MEETING

In social life we are always faced with those among our friends who can't get to any place on time. It seems a great big mystery why they are consistently and dependably late for a lunch, cocktail, or dinner date. They are impervious to hints. Direct comments usually result in total agreement and acknowledgment of the inconvenience, but there are no promises to try to change the never-on-time habit. Some people don't even bother to apologize for being late. Gross social behavior? Certainly! And, too often, you are forced to grin and bear it. In your social community, you may have no choice but to take your friends or guests "as they come." You may not be able to do a thing about it.

In business life, however, we have a somewhat different situation. We do have capabilities for dealing with habitual latecomers. Note, we used the word "capabilities," not abilities. One of the important lessons we learned throughout this book is that you may exercise rank and issue orders to your subordinates to do such and such and get absolutely nowhere. In fact, this style can turn an already poor situation into a very bad one. We learned that authority based on knowledge (A_k) is often equal or superior to authority based on power (Ap). Both are within your reach. One requires skill, while the other comes automatically with the title and the territory.

So, what do you do about a member of your group who is always late in arriving at meetings you've called with plenty of advance notice, or who is slow to return to the meeting room after a coffee break and, thereby, causes delays in start-ups or continuations of work in progress? The sales manager of one company field-tested several approaches: (1) he made jokes about being late (e.g., he will have to live forever because he can't get to his funeral on time); (2) he posted a large attendance sheet with the arrival time written in for each person as he entered the meeting room (red ink for latecomers); (3) he bought and presented the latecomer with an outrageously large alarm clock; and (4) he bought and presented him with a small, travel alarm clock (more subtle and more useful).

None of these actions did more than put the spotlight on the one who was habitually and dependably late. This is often exactly the kind of recognition for overtly benign behavior that the person hungers for. Each of the above efforts will fail, as they did in this case. An unreasonable spotlight-type of recognition is among that person's needs. It is totally improper for him to try to satisfy the need at the expense of his peers and his manager. There are, quite realistically, limits to which peers and manager should be pressed. It is not always possible to satisfy ego needs, no matter how superb the manager might be in his abilities to understand and work with the complexities of human behavior. While it is important to be people oriented, there are tasks that have to be done by the work group. In this case, one person appears to be frustrating the needs of others in the group. The effective manager is concerned with all needs.

This problem was finally solved in a unique way. The sales manager's logic was similar to that used by theater managers: "No one will be seated during the performance." If you've gone to the theater and arrived late, you know that the doors were closed promptly when the performance began and you had to wait for an intermission to find your seat. It seems to work quite well for large crowds of theatergoers. It worked quite well for the latecoming sales man in this example and his frustrated sales manager.

The next notice sent by the sales manager stated that the meeting will start *promptly* at such and such a time. At exactly the announced time, the meeting room door was closed and locked from the inside. The latecomer showed up as usual at a disrespectful time to find the door securely locked and a neatly lettered sign taped to it. The sign read: "Meeting in progress. Please do not disturb or try to enter until the coffeebreak." The sales man cooled his heels for an hour and a half, waiting for the door to be unlocked. His embarrassment and humility were visible—for the first time. It is reported he was one of the first to arrive at the next session. The subject of his previous lateness did not require discussion.

SALESMAN/CUSTOMER CONFICTS

Will Rogers may never have met a man he didn't like, or so say the romantic reports. However, many buyers will tell you they have met sales people they didn't like. Conversely, many sales people feel the same way about some buyers. Usually, this personal and subjective dislike is controlled by both parties. It may remain at a low level. Sometimes it never even comes to the attention of the sales manager. If it is a problem, it is a minor one that seems to regulate itself. Nonetheless, the prudent manager does spend time in the field with his sales people, observing and watching for many things, including personality conflicts that may never appear in a sales report or that never get to the department's complaint desk.

In the specific example we will now discuss, we make the assumption that the sales man has good rapport with most of his customers and his productivity level is satisfactory. There

has never been any hint of personality problems with customers. However, on one of your field trips with him, you
concentrate on calling on major accounts that have reduced
their buying activities with your company, that the sales
man's efforts have not yet successfully penetrated, or that
have made the rare complaint that they dislike doing business with this particular sales person. You go on a "fishing
expedition" and you catch yourself some "fish."

There it is, plain as can be. The tension between your
sales man and the buyer is quite apparent to you. They are
incapable of communicating with each other. Each is ready
to disagree with the other, and neither one is really listening to the other. Each is trying to force his ideas (mostly
opinions) on the other. At stake is a neat order, possibly a
long-term contract for your department. Despite the good
bonuses and commissions your sales man could make, he
argues openly with the potential buyer. On the other hand,
the buyer's company truly needs your company's goods.
Specifications, price, delivery, and benefits are right. But, the
buyer argues and doesn't make a move toward a requisition
or purchase order. This is no way to run a railroad. What
should you do?

You can't take sides—not openly, at any rate. It would be
inappropriate since both parties are really at fault. If you side
with your sales man, the buyer will probably transfer some
of his animosity and hostility to you and the company whose
management you represent. If you side with the buyer, your
sales man will feel that you aren't supporting him but are
letting him down. This begins to look like a no-win situation
for you and your company. You can't have that. You have to
put this train back on the track. And, it's nice to know that
there is a strategy that might work in everybody's favor.

Avoid creating a confrontation unless you are an expert at
diplomacy. Even experts have been known to blow it when a
situation has reachd the argumentative and discordant stage
that this relationship has. The appropriate approach is to
keep your cool, and give everybody else time to cool off as

well. Unless things have reached the shouting and name-calling stage (not likely or you would have heard about it sooner), this cooling-off period should be a short one.

In the meantime, you will discuss your objective view of how to handle this matter with your sales man, recognizing the personalities involved and reminding him of the potential volume of business this buyer controls. The sales man certainly doesn't want to lose any potential commissions, but his foible is that of all human beings—he has a set of emotions; he's not made of stone. You will note that the buyer has the same set of foibles. Suggest that a third party should intervene temporarily at this time. It looks like you are the candidate most likely to succeed. You will, with the agreement of your sales man, personally handle this account (without declaring it a "house account") until the order is written. However, your sales man will accompany you on all visits to the buyer. This demonstrates that he has not been removed from the scene, but implies he has your confidence even though you are in control.

At the appropriate time, when ruffled feathers have been smoothed and egos have been satisfied, you will withdraw from direct participation. You will make it clear, however, to both the sales man and the buyer, that you are available if you are needed.

You might have rearranged the territories. Many frustrated sales managers do try, unsuccessfully, to match each and every customer and sales man. However, the implication of a win-lose solution is inherent in such a maneuver. And, in selling, a win-lose situation can become a lose-lose solution—*nobody wins.* But in the above approach nobody loses and *everybody wins.*

OVERSELLING THE PRODUCT OR SERVICE

Certainly you've had this experience. After the sale is closed and the product or service has been delivered, the customer complains angrily that the "thing (or the service) I got doesn't do what I was told it would do!" Customer service brings the matter to your attention for investigation. What did the customer expect? What was he led to expect? What was he told? Is the product quality, size, or quantity being challenged? Was the service delivered too late, too soon, or incomplete?

The last resort, in a complaint situation, is to take back product, refunding the cost of the goods or services. This is not to say that one must never do these things. Such a hard-and-fast rule, if rigidly observed, will certainly lead to more serious consequences in customer relations and follow-on orders. Good judgment is always required. However, in order to exercise good judgment it is essential to have all the facts on hand.

Who was the sales man on this account? This is your first question after you have heard the details of the customer's complaint. You ask the sales man for his side of the story, trying to maintain objectivity in your search for facts. Someone said "there are always two sides to every story—until you take one of the two sides yourself." You want to avoid this pitfall. Have you had this sort of problem before with the very same sales man? Is a pattern developing which indicates too many of his customers seem to be disappointed? Even if this is a first-time case for this particular sales man, you want to know exactly what the details of the conversation were between the sales man and the customer.

You are searching for indications that the sales man might have made commitments or comments about the company's products, policies, or services that overstated the facts. It is entirely possible that the sales man, in his eagerness to close the order, lost his perspective. A temporary aberration, perhaps, but harmful to everyone involved. More than likely, there is a weakness in the sales man's knowledge of the company's product, service, or policies. This is a danger which the effective sales manager is always alert to, especially when there has been a modification or an introduction of a new product, policy or service.

The indicators here are: (1) additional training is required for this specific sales man; and/or (2) additional or improved sales tools, such as specification sheets, catalogs, brochures, letters, or memoranda, are required for distribution to customers. This may have been a set of circumstances in which the sales man thought he knew his company's product, policies, and services, but, in reality, misunderstood them. *(Note: We are making the assumption the customer was right and the fault is internal to your operation. We will not become involved, in this example, with how you solve the problem at the customer level because we are dealing only with internal situations.)*

It is entirely possible that others in the group are in need of additional training or require new or additional sales tools. A quick survey is conducted of the individual sales people. Fundamental, direct questions are asked—such as:

Are you comfortable with your knowledge of the new product (policy or service)?

Do you have any questions at all about the new product (policy or service)?

Any thoughts on how to improve them?

Are the sales tools appropriate? Are they complete (or incomplete).

How can we help you sell?

What questions are your customers and prospects asking concerning the new products (policies or services)?

How are you answering their questions?

Are they satisfied with your answers?

Are you satisfied with your answers?

The discussions and comments that will follow this line of questioning will be exceptionally revealing to you. If there seems to be confusion, wide variances, or disagreement among your sales people in their responses to these basic questions, then an internal problem does exist. And if so, it would be wise to implement corrective actions—plan and implement more or better training and prepare more or improved sales tools. If it appears that the problem is not widespread but centers on one person or a small number of people in the group, take time to retrain or reeducate these individuals.

The cost of training, or retraining, is often less than the cost of the potential harm or negative impressions that can be generated out in the field among customers who may feel they have been oversold—that they didn't get what they were led to expect. In the meantime, as far as the external matter is concerned, follow company policy in changing this dissatisfied customer to a satisfied customer. If the policy is inadequate to enable you to achieve customer satisfaction, bear in mind that it is not unusual for the books of "exceptions to the rules" to be larger than the rule books themselves. The sales man sold the product, policy, or services as he understood them. It is difficult to label this as "a mistake." Certainly, it was not dishonesty or incompetence. It was an unfortunate incident. You won't try to blame anyone. Remember, when you clench your fist and point an accusing finger, four of your fingers are pointing in your own direction.

EXPENSE ACCOUNT INTELLIGENCE

Everybody loves a new-order report. Nobody likes a new-expense report. You always thank your sales man for bringing in a new order. It is doubtful, however, that you ever thanked him for bringing in a new expense. Yet, properly used, expense reports contain useful information beyond the purely numerical-financial data. A close reading of a sales man's expense report comparing previous expenses for the same territory and examining for recurrent expenses, such as frequent lunches with the *same* customers or prospects, can provide valuable clues to work habits that may be undesirable. Some of these work habits can also account for drops in sales for a sales man who heretofore was a top producer.

We are not suggesting industrial espionage or witch-hunting. The information that can be obtained should be used constructively or not at all. The approach to the examination of expense account reports should not be that of searching for "cheating" or "loading" of expenses. If this has been your approach, whether done by you personally or by a member of your administrative staff, you do not have much confidence in your people. Very likely, they sense this and don't care too much for you as a boss.

You are not searching for ways to make trouble or to give any of your people a hard time. The assumption is that every expense is valid—no "kiting" or falsified numbers. If there is a disagreement with an expense item, consider it a disagreement in judgment of the value of the item—not of its honesty.

Now it has come to your attention that one of your sales men has lunch every Thursday with the same person, a good customer. Is it habit or good business? It has also come to your attention that he has cocktails every Tuesday with another person, and plays golf every Wednesday with still another. Is he a social butterfly or good sales man? Good, pragmatic logic is at play on your part. This sales man has 30 or more accounts—some active, some dormant, others are potential customers. Yet, three of the "social customer" events of each week are with the same people. Rarely do any other account names appear on the expense reports. Looking back into the file of his expense reports, you find this practice has been going on for some time. You know the names of all of his account people. You have met, personally, all of the key people at his 30 or so accounts. For the most part they are pleasant people, but with the usual sprinkling of grouches, gripers, and bad tempers. Still, despite personalities, they represent orders and shipments for the company and handsome bonuses and commissions all around.

Why are they excluded from the business and promotion expense account?

A field trip with your sales man, timed for the middle of the week when he has his usual round of lunch/golf/cocktails, in which you make it clear you want to participate this time, reveals the simple reason for this behavior. You observe he has an excellent relationship and a superb rapport with these three people who represent a small percentage of his total number of accounts.

You are reminded of "Pareto's Law," popularly known as the *80:20 rule*, which contends that 80% of our times is spent in accomplishing only 20% of the results. The converse would also hold true. If Pareto's Law were at work here, you would rationalize that 20% of the salesman's accounts should produce 80% of the territory's sales volume. However, continuing our case study, you did your homework and you know these three account for a very small share of the territory's volume. The degree of attention and the expenses incurred "servicing" these three accounts do not seem justified in your "bean-counting" mind, and you know that your sales man knows this. So, why does he do it?

You offset the visits with these three accounts with visits to as many of the others as possible. Of course, your sales man is with you on each of these calls and, following your suggestion, he is leading the conversation. These are *his* sales calls. You are an interested observer from headquarters who will not try to play boss or dominate the action during these calls. Can you guess what you saw?

The relationship between your sales man and these accounts varied from good to very poor. No conflicts or hostilities were observed during your meetings with the account people. Yet, at best, none was as friendly or as warm as the three whose names have been appearing so often in the expense reports. You gained the clear impression that your sales man didn't try very hard to win the friendship, or at least develop a cordial relationship, of the majority of his accounts. Perhaps he did try hard at one time and didn't succeed. So, he gave up and merely made routine sales calls hoping for an order. He wasn't *selling* the majority of the accounts; he was *taking orders* when they were offered. What's at play here? Let's examine the sales man's probable motivation.

We all have the need for affiliation and identification. This need demands satisfaction. It is especially strong among sales people who work out in the field, pretty much on their own, with relatively little contact with their peers or superiors. Those at the home office have little difficulty joining the society of their associates, identifying with the section, department, division, or company. They are in each other's company every day or almost every day. The know who and where they are. Ignoring office politics and the usual individual dislikes and enmities, desk-bound people, for the most part, do not have the societal-affiliational problems of the soloist in the field. How do many field sales people satisfy this need?

Some do it through a concentration on selling during the day and doing their thing at night, weekends, and holidays. They join business clubs and participate in other societal activities—for example, Rotary, Kiwanis, Lions, Elks, church functions, fund raising for nonprofit associations, fraternities, societies, professional associations, avocation or hobby circles, and the country club. There, they may find people they like and who, reciprocally, may like them. They meet with them under circumstances that are comfortable, friendly, and risk free. In this way, their strong needs for friendship, affiliation, and identification are satisfied.

Geographical separation may make it difficult for the field sales man to affiliate or identify with the company or his boss. This is his lot. Some cope with it more successfully than others, of course. In the example we are reviewing, the sales man has created his own small circle of friends. True, his personal need for friendship is overriding the need of the company and your own need as the manager.

You may have missed the clues or messages he has been sending you all along. For example, remember how angry you got with him when he defended his customers against the company in several disputes over products or promises? Remember how often you asked yourself, "Who does he work for anyway? The company or his customers?" The questions were quite rhetorical. They weren't really questions. More likely they were challenges, trains of your own thoughts. You always tried to find a way to cool off so you could tell him, "Remember where your paycheck comes from!" However, he might have responded, "From the same place yours comes from—our customers!" So, you prudently avoided a shootout and a showdown in the sales corral.

Yes, the clues and the messages were being sent to you all along. The sender was on the right frequency; the receiver was not. Okay, now we know that you are part of the problem. How do you become part of the solution? How do you help this sales man develop a sense of affiliation and identification with the company? It won't happen overnight. It will take time and understanding on your part. But, it can be done. It has to be done, and here's the way to do it:

1.   After recognizing the symptoms, analyzing the problem, and confirming your conclusions through personal observation, discuss with him, during a field trip, the need to foster better relationships with his other accounts in a professional effort to improve the sales volume for his territory. You will express admiration for the fine relationship he has with his three regulars, and suggest that he apply the same social skills in the direction of his other accounts. This defines the problem and the objective.

2.   Suggest that you would like him to come to the home office (or wherever your office is, if you are a district or regional manager) for several days. The stated reason is to

bring him up to date on products, policies, and procedures. You will do this in a way that precludes inferences on his part that the visit contains threats to his security. In fact, the purpose of the visit is quite the opposite and no threats are involved whatsoever. He should be made aware that this is a positive step for him and for the territory and that when he returns to the field and his territory you and he will have a better understanding of how the office can help him do his job in the field.

3. You will spend more time in the field with him than you have been doing. The objective is to help him cross the invisible barriers that seem to have arisen between him and a number of his accounts. Sometimes, all a hostile buyer needs is evidence that the sales person is supported by and has a direct channel of communications with the home office. Your visit can provide this evidence.

Once more, everybody wins!

COMMANDS CONFUSED WITH REPORTS

Or, is it the other way around—reports confused with commands? The problem has been puzzling you for some time. You give orders or instructions to your people and they do not respond in the way you expect them to. For example, at 10:00 A.M. you give an order to one of your district managers to have his new-business forecast in your office by 3:00 this afternoon. At 3:30 you still haven't received the forecast and you are beginning to get aggravated. You don't like to have your orders disobeyed. When you said 3:00, you meant it because you have to consolidate the district manager's data with other forecasts and develop an integrated forecast to deliver to the financial manager first thing the next morning. You don't take pleasure in the fact that, even if the district manager's forecast had been delivered on time at 3:00, you would still have to "burn the oil" at your desk until midnight. Now that he is late, you don't know how you can fulfill your own commitment.

Why does it seem that in order to get anything done on time you have to do it yourself? Something's got to be done about all this insubordination—people ignoring your orders and doing just as they please! What has happened to the old-fashioned work ethic? Don't people care anymore? What happened to pride in a job well done?

It is possible that everyone is out of step but you? Is this likely to be true, though? Probably not. Perhaps the fault is with your style of communication rather than with your staff. Perhaps you get the same feeling at home—in your own castle you are not the king. You have the same problem with your family. You tell your teenager, as he heads out the front door, "It's raining outside!" He says, "Right" and continues out the door without a raincoat. You grumble, "That kid never listens to me!" Ah, but he did listen to you. You reported to him that it was raining outside and he responded with a word of agreement. Isn't this true? You are frustrated, even angry, because he didn't put on his raincoat or take an umbrella. Your intention was to have him put on a raincoat or take an umbrella. However, that isn't at all what you said. You thought you were issuing a *command*, but you gave a *report*.

Do you do the same thing at work? Give reports when you mean to give commands?

Let's review the command you thought you gave to your district manager. You may have said, as you ended the conversation with him, "I need to start work on my consolidated forecast for the financial manager at 3:00." He may have said, "Right." You may have assumed you gave him an order or instruction to have his forecast on your desk by 3:00 P.M., but you didn't. You gave him a report on your work schedule. You may lose the argument that "anyone with half an intelligence should have known what I meant." The district manager was probably thinking about all the forecasts he has to collect from his field-sales people so that he can prepare his own consolidation, which you had originally scheduled for completion and delivery to you a day later. The schedule apparently had been changed, but you did not issue a new command. You merely reportd on your own timetable.

Here's another common example. In a discussion with one of your staff members, a problem was revealed that called for an immediate group conference. As your staff member leaves your office, both of you obviously concerned with the seriousness of the situation, you state, "We'd better have a staff meeting and resolve this matter!" He says, "Right." You clear your desk and tell your secretary to hold all calls during the staff meeting.

Now two things go haywire. First, the staff does not come to your office immediately for a meeting. In fact, you have to call them to find out where they are and why they are not in your office. They are surprised to hear you say you had called a meeting. You are surprised that they are surprised. Second, when the meeting finally gets going, your secretary does not hold calls but puts them through to you until you impatiently say, "Didn't I tell you to hold all calls during the staff meeting?" Normally, she is a very effective secretary, so she is surprised at your manner. She didn't know this was a staff meeting. You always have your staff meetings on Monday morning and today is Wednesday.

Did you actually command that a staff meeting be held immediately? Or, did you report that there had better be one? A problem in human communications, of course. In business, at play, or in the home, it is easy to miscommunicate—easy to confuse reports with commands. Be careful, please! (Is this last comment a report or a command?)

BRAINSTORMING VERSUS ARGUING

"Hey! Let's brainstorm this one!" The word "brainstorm" has now become a verb. We brainstorm for ideas, new products, and innovation. The concept of the "brainstorm meeting" is reported to have been created by an advertising agency executive. He periodically called his staff into a conference room and presented them with important problems, such as the need for new advertising slogans, themes, or campaigns.

Usually for no more than one hour at a time, the selected staff members would give free rein to their off-the-top-of-the-head thinking. The thoughts and ideas were to come out rapidly, to be voiced without deep thought or analysis. The *quantity* of ideas was emphasized in the expectation that *quality* would follow. Ideas were not evaluated at the moment they were expressed, out of concern that any criticism might discourage free thinking. Negative statements were rigidly and strictly forbidden. This was a rule that was enforced instantly. Transgressors were unceremoniously evicted from the brainstorming session and, if the individual was repeatedly negative, he might never be invited to participate again.

Every idea was recorded (by hand, in those days before the cassette recorder). After the meeting was over, a select few, usually people who had not attended the brainstorming session, acted as the evaluation committee. Thus, many ideas were generated. Although most were rejected by the committee, the results usually proved that the time and effort were worthwhile investments.

Brainstorming is a technique for problem solving. It is not intended to be and should not be used as a platform for egoistic personalities. It is not a competition. It is a team effort. A stimulus of creativity is injected into the group and it spreads rapidly, instantly infecting the participants with a positive and wholesome "virus." The concept has spread throughout American industry. Sometimes it works and sometimes it fails. The paragraphs which follow describe a common reason for failure.

Unfortunately, some participants who are innately aggressive may try to dominate the session. They have fixed views. They are inflexible in their thinking. Their way is not only the best way, it is the one and only way. Thus, they may instantly and callously "pooh-pooh" the thoughts that others express. They are specialists in put-down techniques, being sarcastic and vitriolic. What was intended to be a creative problem-solving session rapidly deteriorates into a do-nothing, get-nowhere battle of egos.

Why is this allowed to happen? Some managers do not understand basic principles of brainstorming as described on the preceding page. They believe in establishing battle bunkers, that internal competition is a healthy thing, and that any hard feelings that surface will soon dissipate. Right on one count! Internal competition that is *competently managed* can be very healthy. By this we mean, in part, that personality conflicts are to be excluded and precluded from the performance of the tasks. Wrong on one count! Hard feelings that surface in the brainstorming session are counter-productive and rapidly destroy any possibility of deriving benefits from the time and energy that are dedicated to the session. Hard feelings belong outside the conference room.

Those managers who understand the proper practice of brainstorming watch closely for any negativism and egoistic displays. The moment it surfaces, they squelch it! There is no time for long and drawn-out explanations or idealistic approaches. A typical squelch can be in the form of a question: "Pardon me, Joe (or Tom, or Dick, or Harry). Is that a positive approach you are taking? Sounds negative to me, so let's move right along." This is not a put-down, but a type of stopper that serves to rapidly restore the meeting to a positive and constructive level.

Whether or not these meetings are called "brainstorming sessions" or by any other favorite or popular name is not important. Just think about the many times you've seen problem-solving meetings go down the drain because somebody chose to argue an idea that was proposed by someone else. Consider how the situation was handled or mishandled at the time. If you are the chairman of the next brainstorming session, prepare yourself to firmly but nicely put a quick stopper on argumentative behavior. The effective brain-stormer is a team player. Even though an individual partici-pant may usually be a loner or a soloist, when he plays on the team in this game *everybody is equal* and *everybody is a winner!*

19 EVERYTHING YOU ALWAYS WANTED TO KNOW ABOUT MOTIVATION

. . . According to
Vroom, Freud,
Herzberg, and Maslow

"Theory? That's for college professors! I'm a practical guy. I work at managing sales people." This is an argument typical of many high-energy sales managers. It is likely they secretly fear or have closed their minds to the possibility that there are common denominators that can be used to define—and possibly predict—the behavior of sales people under a given set of circumstances. Such managers were probably highly energetic in their youth. They were, most certainly, highly energetic as sales people. There's nothing wrong with all of this, except that they probably know a great deal about how to work hard but next to nothing about how to "work smart."

"Theory" is defined in many ways. The definition that

appeals most of all is "a plausible, scientifically acceptable general principle or body of principles offered to explain phenomena that lead to systematic procedures as a basis of action." Chew on and digest this one for a moment.

It is generally agreed that people are the most complex of all things. Therefore, they cannot be reduced to a bunch of on/off switches, as in an electrical control panel, to make things happen or not happen. But man, in his finite wisdom and infinite curiosity, is engaged in a continuous and endless search for easy labels and short answers to the numerous questions and riddles about his own species. He correctly rejects the view that says, "Oh well, that's the way it is—live with it!"

In an effort to explain the riddles of human behavior, a body of principles has been developed, published, and widely circulated that tends to explain the phenomena of human behavior. The body of principles, the multiplicity of theories, and the numerous names of leading behavioral scientists and theorists provide prolific evidence of the fact that there are many answers to the question "What makes man tick the way he does?"

Of course, as long as man remains as complex as he is, the theories will continue to be created, expounded, tried, revised, accepted, and rejected. The pressures exerted on the sales manager often force him to search for instant solutions to all people-problems. Talk about resistance to change, rigid thinking, and the same solution for all problems, a sales manager can be as guilty as anyone else in this regard. How neat it would be to be able to instantly find the switch that turns people on to high levels of motivation and productivity. At the moment, the word "productivity" seems to be more popular than the word "motivation." For our purposes, "motivation" and "productivity," though not identical in meaning, are inseparable. "Motivation," in our usage, includes the cause of a human action or series of actions that produce a change in output. If the output is positive (e.g., causes an increase in orders and/or an improvement in interpersonal relationships—especially the former), it is referred to in terms of "productivity." It has become popular to infer and imply that *any change in productivity is always positive.*

When we wonder about what motivates any individual, we are expressing curiosity about what turns him on. As you might have guessed, "turns him on" is not a technical expression. You may never hear it used in a conclave of behavioral scientists. It is rarely used in professorial dissertations, tutorial papers, or educators' journals. But it sure does make the point among the pragmatists, and sales managers are known to be especially pragmatic about such things.

Nevertheless, it is useful, illuminating, and helpful to learn and discuss several of the leading theories. It's useful, because theory can add new meaning to the practice of managing sales people; illuminating, because it can throw a bright light into a dark and mysterious corner of the human mind; helpful, because a good foundation of theory helps us recognize behavioral patterns as familiar phenomena rather than strangely complex, foreign, and frightening experiences. Knowledge of some of the theories of behavior enables us to do our jobs constructively by maintaining the work situation as a familiar, friendly, and nonthreatening environment. Theory provides us with possible explanations for the behavior of sales people trying to perform under the pressures of the sales tasks. These explanations can help the sales manager accurately predict human responses to a specified set of circumstances. Certainly, they can assist in defining the nature of a specific, undesirable situation in which human behavior, or misbehavior, plays a leading role.

Having developed a definition of the problem and the circumstances, the sales manager with a good foundation in the theory of behavior is most likely ahead of the game. He should find himself in the satisfying position of being able to develop a course of action that will bring about a change or a series of positive changes, either by modifying his game plan or by bringing about modifications in human behavior. The course selected will then have an extraordinarily high probability for success in achieving the desired results of positive motivation, restored or increased productivity levels, and reduced or minimized open conflict.

Please note that we have used the expression "reduced or minimized conflict." We deliberately avoided the expression "eliminated conflict." It is a belief held by many behavioral scientists, and a belief we share, that conflict is the inevitable *and* desirable product of an environment in which high achievers and creative people are brought together as part of a group effort to attain quantifiable results. It is desirable because it is an indicator that creative juices are flowing, that ideas are being developed, and that innovative thinking is seeking an outlet. However, conflict must be managed to assure that no blocks are created in this search for a productive outlet.

It is a virtual anomaly that the sales manager aggressively recruits and hires highly individualistic sales people who have track records as high producers, and then thrusts them into a group environment that implicitly attempts to reform their personalities and behavioral patterns to conform to the team's mold, format, and configuration. This sales manager is too often unprepared for the interpersonal conflicts that develop quickly, sometimes explosively. He may try physically separating people by reassigning or transferring them from one territory to another as he tries to break up the conflict. Too soon, however, new interpersonal conflicts appear. And, once again, the sales manager is frustrated. The problem has not been solved. It has only been shifted geographically or temporarily driven underground.

An alternative to an environment fraught with people whose ideas, concepts, and business thoughts are in open conflict is mediocrity (offering, at best, a superficially stable ambience of contentment). Although it may enable the manager to boast "I run a happy ship," the types of people who choose to stay may bring about business results that are quite unimpressive. Suppressing conflict, "because it upsets my people," is undesirable and even dangerous. It can bring about a serious frustration of needs and inspire hostile actions among those whose attempts to express their ideas, concepts, and viewpoints are blocked. In a sales-oriented activity, the high achievers may quickly tire of the "happy ship." They may restlessly seek a new environment—one in which they find compassion and understanding; one that appreciates and accommodates their individuality; one that recognizes their unwillingness to accept other's ideas and concepts at face value; one that offers the opportunity to challenge their peers and even, at times, their superiors. Many times, this seeking and searching causes interpersonal conflicts. And, the inability to constructively manage conflict may very well be one of the major causes of failure among sales managers.

The sales manager who is not skilled in the management of conflict begins to feel like the sorcerer's apprentice. He chops the broom into two parts, then four parts. To his amazement and horror, the original problem escalates exponentially. It is not solved. In fact, he finds himself on a treadmill, developing what appear to be excellent solutions which don't work very well! They don't work very well because the solutions don't match the problems. The definitions were quite imperfect—usually based on a "gut feeling" and previous experience that may not relate to the present.

The question is often asked, "What is the *best* management style?" Underlying the question is the wish for a simplified formula for successfully dealing with all situations. The answer to this question is not simple. The best management style is the one that is appropriate to the specific situation. This implies there is no such thing as a bad style. No such implication is intended. The direct statement is made that *any style that is inappropiately applied is bad and any style that is appropriately applied is good.*

For example, at the start of a major task, when all assignments have been made and roles have been clarified for the individual participants, a *laissez-faire* style may be quite appropriate—for the short term. Lay off. Keep the pressure off individuals and the group. Allow each member time to form and find himself. Enable the group to develop its character. This is total people orientation. However, if allowed to continue indefinitely it can also become an abdication of managerial responsibility and accountability.

Then, there are times when an *authoritarian* style must be brought into play. For example, as time passes, pressure may have to be applied on the group and its individual members to ensure that they are still on the right course with respect to meeting their objectives. If the group or any of its members has drifted off course, the style of the manager must flex again. In accordance with deadlines and goals, the manager's style may move to and from total authoritarianism (which is total task orientation); to and from an inspirational, collaborative and democratic captain-of-the-ship mode (which strikes a balance between people and tasks); and to and from the laissez-faire style (which leaves people to their own devices). The message transmitted in this paragraph is intended to reinforce the view that there is no style that is right and no style that is wrong. The style must be examined within the context of the situation. It is neither *appropriate* nor *inappropriate,* neither *right* nor *wrong.* Now, let's hear from some of the best-known behavioral scientists.

A GOOD PLACE TO START

Victor H. Vroom, Professor of Industrial Administration and Psychology at the Carnegie Institute of Technology, has put in writing an interesting concept of work and motivation. Although it was probably not Professor Vroom's direct intention, his concept or theory seems quite applicable to sales people. This includes the stimuli that are applied to them by their environments (and, we add, their supervisors) and the responses that are elicited (in terms of performance). There are some who believe that people seek rather than avoid stimulation. Convert the word "stimulation" to the word "incentive" and the thought becomes clearer; that is, *under some circumstances*, incentives can strengthen responses. In fact, environments and supervisors who do not provide stimulation or incentives create a set of working conditions that most people find highly unpleasant. However, while a particular set of conditions or a specific incentive may appear to be desirable, the behavioral scientist, as well as the pragmatic sales manager, has yet to discover a way to accurately predict or forecast the degrees of pleasure or pain that will be generated. This does not mean that job reinforcement is a doubtful personnel management tool. Quite the opposite; if we deal in probabilities, it is better to have tried reinforcement techniques and incentives than never to have tried them at all.

Professor Vroom makes use of the word "valence" in describing his concept of human responses to stimuli. The response is relevant to the attainment of a defined outcome, objective, or the result of an input-level of effort. As he wrote, "For the sake of consistency, we use the term 'valence' in referring to affective orientations toward particular outcomes." In the systems to which Professor Vroom refers, an outcome is positively valent when the person prefers attaining it to not attaining it. An outcome has a valence of zero when the person is indifferent to attaining it; and is negatively valent when the individual prefers not attaining it to attaining it.

One of the difficulties the sales manager faces in planning an incentive program is that of making the rules equitable for each member of the sales group who participates. The difficulty is related to the valence of the outcome and the value of the outcome to the individual. A person may desire an objective or a reward but derive little satisfaction from attaining it; or, he may try to avoid an objective, a specific sales contest which, later on, he finds to be very satisfying. Often, there is considerable discrepancy between the anticipated satisfaction that might be derived from an outcome (valence) and the actual satisfaction (value) that it provides.

As every sales manager or supervisor learns through experience, there are many outcomes that are positively or negatively valent to sales people. The strength of a sales person's desire or aversion to the outcomes is not always based on the intrinsic properties of the reward, but on the anticipated satisfaction or dissatisfaction associated with other outcomes to which they are expected to lead. Some people join group activities, such as country clubs or after-hour company recreational teams, because they believe that such memberships will enhance their status in their specific communities. Or, they may earnestly want to perform their jobs more effectively in the expectation that a superior level of performance can lead to a promotion.

The specific outcomes that a sales person may attain are dependent on choices that he makes and on other circumstances that are beyond his control. For example, the sales person who calls on a specific customer under highly competitive conditions is seldom certain that he will get the order. As all managers and sales people know, the majority of decision-making situations involve risk-taking. Any time an individual chooses between alternatives which involve the risk of uncertainty, his behavior is affected by his confidence in the probability of the outcome of each of the alternatives, and by his preferences among the alternative outcomes. Psychologists refer to these responses as *expectancies*. This is defined as a belief concerning the likelihood that a particular act will be followed by a particular outcome. A maximal-strength expectancy is the subjective certainty that the act will be followed by the expected outcome. Minimal- or zero-strength expectancy is indicated by the subjective certainty that the act will not be followed by the desired outcome. Expectancy is an association of action and outcome. Behavior on an individual's part is, some theorists hold, the result of a field of forces, each of which has direction and magnitude. If the direction and magnitude are toward the individual, the valence or attractiveness is high and positive.

In postulating and expounding his theories—remember,

many theories are born of observation of phenomena and often state those things many sales managers are aware of but have not been able to articulate—Vroom clarifies some of the mysteries of the behavior of sales people (for example, their responsiveness or unresponsiveness to sales promotions, contests, quotas, "spiffs," bonuses, and other expressed, implied, or inferred promises of material reward). As Vroom writes, "One indisputable source of the desire of people to work is the money they are paid for working." However, despite the cliché that says "money can't buy happiness," it is a totally viable medium of exchange for many of the physical and material items which are necessary for survival and comfort. For those who care to investigate the theories of Victor Vroom further, we recommend his book, *Work and Motivation.** But, for the moment, let's investigate some of the relevant theories of a psychologist/psychiatrist whose name is quite well-known but whose theories are often misunderstood or misquoted—Dr Sigmund Freud.

WE CALL ON FREUD

A couch isn't needed; we'll make this "call" standing up. It is usual, in any discussion of the phenomena of human behavior, to hear the name Freud frequently mentioned, referenced, and praised or belittled. In cocktail conversation, the references are invariably directed, with snickers, at sex-oriented humor. Dr. Freud was anything but a dirty old man. He is considered by many to be the father of psychoanalysis and personality theory. We have no way of knowing how successful he might hve been as a sales manager. We have never heard the subject argued or debated, although it is worthy of a debate that matches the theorist against the pragmatist. Based on the controversial nature of the man and his theories, he probably would not have been very success-

* Victor Vroom, *Work and Motivation* (New York: Wiley, 1964).

ful as a sales man. But, there is little doubt that he would have been enormously successful as a teacher and guide for those who had the responsibility for leading others through the sales profession. Although not necessarily so, several of his theories, now known as *principles,* appear to have been developed through the observation of people at work in the selling profession. Let's briefly examine several of these principles and note how they tend to match the characteristics of many of the sales types you have known.

The Pleasure Principle

As many human behaviorists—and sales managers, for that matter—have observed, man (i.e., the human species) is a pleasure-seeking animal. He will "go to great pains" to avoid pain. Freud contended that man's every act is motivated by the desire for pleasure and, to some degree, by the avoidance of pain. It may come as new information to many of us that Freud was a highly moral individual. His use of the word "pleasure" was not at all intended in the hedonistic sense. Freud's intention was to describe pleasure as a sense of living in a pleasant state of being, making efforts to avoid whatever is the opposite of pleasure; or, if not succeeding in these efforts, attempting to reduce the negative sensations. Freud held that the search for pleasure is instinctive in all animals.

This, to some degree, tends to explain the fact that high-achieving sales people usually are not risk takers. While they may talk about "challenge" and "beating out the competition," it is so painful for them to lose to the competition or to fail to close a sale that many will avoid a situation in which they do not have an even chance, a 50/50 opportunity, of winning. The less experienced sales people, the hot young tigers, are the ones who will tackle the world of competition without first weighing the odds, as do those who have been through the unforgettable pain of past failure.

The Reality Principle

One of the responsibilities of being a human being, is awareness of the many societal rules and limits imposed by the community in which one lives and works. The reality principle is a learned process, as compared with the pleasure principle which is instinctive. As man progress from the totally self-centered infant stage to adulthood, he learns that he must occasionally put off or delay the fulfillment of an immediate pleasure and anticipate a pleasure that may be even greater at some future time. "Let the little ones get away—go after the big orders!"

Sometimes, a problem is imposed on the sales manager by a sales person who is not aware of the reality principle and thinks only in terms of immediate gratification and pleasure. You will recognize that this is also known as immaturity or childishness, both of which can be forgiven in an infant. They are annoying, however, when manifested in the behavioral pattern of an adult.

The Tension-Reduction Principle

Conflict is similar to two or more forces operating in opposing directions. Physical objects, when placed under such differing tensions, will exhibit stress and may even fracture or veer in unexpected directions. Freud observed that man cannot avoid the pain of stress when he is being pulled in two opposite directions, one of which may be the need to fulfill his own desires for pleasure (see "Pleasure Principle" and the other may be the boundaries of reality (see "Reality Principle"). These oppositions of instinctive and learned behavior create stress and, at times, unpredictable behavior on the part of the man. Stress is painful and usually has a negative effect on interpersonal relationships with peers, superiors, subordinates, and the other individuals with whom one comes in contact. Some can recognize these sensations when they are occurring within themselves and can successfully cope with them. Others are less successful or fail completely, and, thereby, present the sales manager with a problem. There's one more observation made by Dr. Freud that you will most certainly recognize as another problem with which you have had to deal.

The Repetition-Compulsion Principle

"Man is a creature of habit." Freud didn't say it in exactly those words, but he did comment that man is a habit-following animal, inclined to repeat that which is successful. Now, there may not be anything wrong with repeating that which is successful. However, the longer an individual repeats the same thing the more fixed the habit becomes as part of his daily conduct. When this happens, the habit can become so fixed that he may compulsively and repeatedly follow it as a method of dealing with each situation. The difficulty here is that each situation is not necessarily the same as those which precede it. Thus, one solution, regardless of the problem, just doesn't work. And, the sales person who approaches each selling situation with the same solution, whether or not it leads to success, has quite succumbed to a repetition compulsion. This is usually a cause for some concern to the sales manager who recognizes full well that each sales situation must stand on its own merits and, generally, demands its own set of strategic responses.

Ego-Defense Mechanisms

Another topic of conversation at cocktail parties is the set of *ego-defense mechanisms* defined by Freud. There is some argument as to whether or not it was Sigmund Freud or his daughter, a prominent psychiatrist in her own time, who created the definitions. The originator of the definitions is not at all as important as the concept and the content of the set of ego-defense mechanisms and their influence on human behavior. Each member of this "set" has been given a name. It is interesting to note how they typify those people with whom we work on a daily basis.

Repression: When we hold back a strong desire, inhibit a feeling of passion, restrain a powerful impulse, contain an intense rage—when we keep these feelings from being brought to a conscious level of action—we are exercising repression. "Good thing!" you say. Yes, repressing a powerful urge or desire that is potentially dangerous and harmful to others as well as to ourselves is a good thing. But, a price of sorts is often paid for this self-controlled repression. The price is a build-up of tension and stress.

What is it that causes us to repress our impulses, sensations, and angers? Fear—fear of the consequences of unacceptable behavior. What is the effect on the work and performance of individuals who go into repression? Negative, of course. The individuals who repress their strongest feelings are distracted from the objectives of their work assignments. Their work is affected and they often have a negative effect on their peers. Is it better to avoid repression and give full vent to one's true feelings? You might as well ask whether or not mayhem and violence are to be permitted in your office. When the sales manager recognizes that the performance of one of his people is suffering because of a deep hurt or anger, it becomes his special task to find an effective way to relieve the tension and stress. This is not done by telling the sales person to "let go, pal, and follow your instincts." It is done by getting to the heart of the problem and treating the situation as a genuine conflict. The treatment for such situations is given among the many case studies and options discussed in the first 17 chapters of this book.

Regression: Much of Freud's writing deals with regression as an ego-defense mechanism that is concerned with returning to the behavioral characteristics of one's childhood. It is possible, however, as a defense mechanism for the injured ego, to return to another previous period of one's lifetime that does not go as far back as childhood. One can, intellectually and emotionally, return to another period in one's life, even an adult period, in which one found either greater satisfaction or a similar situation offering a potential solution to today's problem.

This may be exhibited by a sales man who, because he is not doing too well lately, spends too much time reliving past victories and great sales experiences: He spends too much time in the past and too little time in resolving the current state of affairs. But the defense of the injured ego is vital to all humans. Regressive behavior is sometimes related to the repetition-compulsion principle wherein the individual tries to relive an old solution in a new situation, hoping to find a way out of the dilemma. Luck rather than skill may play an exaggerated role, and the prudent sales manager is quick to recognize the ego-defense mechanism at work and takes appropriate action.

Projection: Extraordinarily complex on the surface, the depth of this ego-defense mechanism is not great because, when it is at work, it can be recognized quickly by a casual observer. It is natural to want to think well of one's self and not to harbor bad feelings toward one's coworkers. However, it may be equally natural to dislike or even hate a fellow. When this does happen, the individual who holds these feeling of dislike or hatred may feel guilty. He may project his feelings, quite unwittingly, by claiming that the other fellow "hates me." Or, he might express the belief that "those two guys are ganging up on me." In reality, he may very strongly dislike "those two guys" himself, but his ego will not allow him to believe he is capable of such strong feelings of animosity. So, his ego demands a strong defense and an early release from tension. It can be gained through projection.

There are other ego-defense mechanisms postulated and defined by Freud. However, the ones we have described are probably among those most often encountered by the sales manager who finds himself caught up in the urgent need to understand and, thereby, solve people-problems.

HERZBERG OFFERS A TWO-FACTOR THEORY

Frederick Herzberg developed a theory based on a study of accountants and engineers employed in the general area of Pittsburgh, Pennsylvania. These simple directions were given to the participants:

> Think of a time when you felt exceptionally good or exceptionally bad about your job, either your present job or any other job you have had. This can be either the "long-range" or the "short-range" kind of situation, as I have just described it. Tell me what happened.

The responses have been widely published among the community of behavioral scientists. They have been quoted frequently; they have been both challenged and supported. Some claim the sample taken was statistically inadequate to be presented as a meaningful study from which conclusions can be drawn. However, we will present Dr. Herzberg's conclusions and you may judge for yourself the reason why, despite the arguments, many psychologists and laypeople have accepted the logic Dr. Herzberg presents in what is known as the *duality* or *two-factor theory.*

You must first recognize that the question was put only to staff professionals who, as they perform their tasks, must exercise judgment, initiative, and some degree of creativity. Production people, who perform routine and repetitive tasks, were not asked the questions. This enables us to relate the study and its conclusions to sales people and to sales managers. Good feelings, as reported by the respondents, were associated with job experiences and the content of the work that was performed. *Bad* feelings were associated with the physical environment, lack of opportunity for advancement, and other peripheral aspects of the job assignments. For example, good feelings were experienced by one respondent who had been given a highly responsible assignment that was important to the company. He took great pride in the fact that he had been selected for the task in the first place.

In another response, one which engendered bad feelings, the person had been given responsibility for providing back-up for his manager during the manager's absence. All well and good; however, it seems that the manager was always too busy to provide what the respondent felt would be adequate training. In fact, the reporter contended that each time he tried to ask questions in an effort to learn more about what his manager expected of him, the manager would become quite annoyed and impatient. This caused the person to feel intense frustration in trying to do a job for which he had not been given adequate preparation and instruction. He had feelings of being unrecognized and in a dead-end position.

Herzberg defined the two factors in his study as *satisfiers* and *dissatisfiers*. The satisfiers were known as *motivators*. The dissatisfiers were called *hygiene factors*. A dissatisfier is a factor that, if inadequate in quantity and quality, can make a person unhappy, tense, conflict prone, and frustrated. When he becomes aware of this rather personal problem, the manager's task is to attempt to convert a dissatisfier to a satisfier. This effort may include a salary increase, in response to a specific complaint, or a change of office environment, again in response to a statement of dissatisfaction. These actions may reduce the causes of dissatisfaction—hygiene factors—but they do not necessarily motivate the person to improve his performance level. The sales manager who does improve the hygiene factor may note a sudden spurt of interest and action on the part of the sales person: However, it is quite likely that this positive activity will not be sustained in the form of increased productivity.

Those who reported good feelings related them to specific tasks being done as well as the job itself. Bad feelings were recalled when the people felt they had not been treated quite fairly, company policy was poorly administrated or defective, and the work environment was dissatisfying. Here is a listing of dissatisfiers and satisfiers, also respectively referred to as hygiene factors and motivators.

Hygiene Factors (Dissatisfiers and Inadequacies)	Motivators (Satisfiers and Stimulators)
Policies and administration	Achievement
Supervision	Recognition for accomplishments
Working conditions	Challenging work
Money, status, and security	Growth and development opportunity

The statement of a dissatisfier means that the element in that column is negative; for example, poorly administered company policies, unpleasant physical surroundings, low pay, and so on. The conversion of a dissatisfier to a satisfier is not necessarily the simple key to motivation. The absence of dissatisfiers is not a key to motivation either. However, the presence of positive hygiene factors is essential to the effective implementation of the motivators. The effective sales manager understands the need for appropriate hygiene factors as a basis on which to build the motivators. He must give proper guidance, instruction, and support to his sales people. Note that money is at the end of the list. Even if placed under the listing for motivators, money would probably be near the bottom of the list. Motivation is not directly related to the amount of money or other material rewards offered to sales people, as every sales manager learns when he depends exclusively on such rewards as a motivator. Yes, it can work in short spurts, in the short term as we pointed out earlier, as every sales manager who has had to depend on sales contests has learned. There are few if any long-term residual effects gained from a money- or prize-oriented program.

MASLOW DESCRIBES A HIERARCHY OF NEEDS

Abraham Maslow, famed teacher, writer, behavioral scientist and creative thinker, observes the existence of classes of needs and the interrelationships that exist among them. Basically, Maslow contends that man has a series of definable needs that he strives to satisfy. And, as long as a need is not met and is unsatisfied, it remains a motivator, a driving force, or a stimulus to action. Once the need has been satisfied it ceases to be a motivator. Well, let's try a convoluted sort of logic. If the sales manager can find out what the need is that the high-achieving salesman is trying to satisfy, and if the sales manager can frustrate that need (i.e., keep it from being satisfied), the high achiever will continue to achieve. Continuing in this same mode of logic, if the doctor never cures his patient, he is guaranteed a continuous (and profitable) relationship with him. We know this is not the way it works in real life. The professional sales manager strives to encourage and motivate his high achievers to still greater levels of achievement. The doctor endeavors to restore the health of the sick patient. The uniqueness of each, the effectiveness of the sales manager and the good doctor, is related to their individual abilities to recognize symptoms, diagnose the situation, identify the options, select the one option most likely to accurately reflect the sales person and the patient's needs, design a beneficial program, and bring about the appropriate action. With these premises in mind, let's examine this real world about which Maslow theorized in his famous *Hierarchy of Needs.*

Maslow defined an orderly relationship of human needs, both physical and emotional. While he identifies five levels, they are categorized at two major levels: (1) *primary,* or unlearned, needs, with which all animals are born; and (2) secondary, or those needs which are learned as we grow older, gain more experience with life, and become more exposed to the various environments in which we must function.

Primary needs include the *physiological* or *natural* needs—

for food, drink, and sleep. (Other biological functions, of course, are natural and do not have to be learned). Another primary need is for *safety*—for physical shelter and security. Aboriginal and primitive people dedicated their entire lives to satisfying these primary needs. The cave man, motivated by hunger, had to leave the safety of the cave and venture forth, risking his life, in search of food to satisfy that need. Once hunger was overcome, he would feel the need for sleep; when the dominant need once again became hunger, the cycle of search, feed, and sleep would be renewed.

One might allow one's imagination to roam and assume there were leaders among the cave people. The mightiest of hunters was top man on the team or in the cave colony. Possibly, when the meat was brought in for the rock/table, he would receive (or take) the choicest parts for himself. Perhaps he ate it while squatting on a plateau or pillar that put his head at a higher level than all others in the colony. If this is accurate—and we will never know for certain—these were his status symbols, the needs that he learned and acquired. And they demanded satisfaction. Woe unto anyone who challenged his highly placed, though uncushioned, seat.

In modern times as in the past man feels the need to belong to a group. In addition, the need to impress one's business and social associates is ever present. In some this "esteem" need is a stronger, more dominant need than in others. We were not born with a need for a larger car, bigger house, nicer clothes, more professionally landscaped front yard, or longer and wider swimming pool than our neighbors have. We were not born with a need to join a deluxe country club, or with a need to acquire more worldly goods and multiple possessions than are essential for the satisfaction of our primary needs. These needs were learned, acquired through external environments and influences.

The urge to satisfy the primary needs can be so strong that it has no "respect" for the sanctity of the top executive's position or for those at the low end of the business totem pole. Regardless of the urgency or significance of the conference, all must take "breaks" to satisfy natural needs for visits to the restroom or for a refreshment. "Let's break for lunch (or dinner)" is an anticipated recommendation, welcomed by all participants at the appropriate time; the "appropriate time" is when the need for natural refreshments become stronger than the need for discussions and resolutions related to the environment. At such a time, the motivators move rapidly from secondary to primary need satisfaction. Yet, when these primary needs have been satisfied, the secondary needs return to dominate and motivate every individual.

Five Levels of Need

Classically, Maslow's Hierarchy of Needs is diagrammed as a tiered triangle, with the most irresistible of the primary needs at the base. The primary needs are the two lowest levels in the hierarchy. The next three levels are the secondary needs. These are shown in Figure 1.

Level 1.   Physiological/natural. Described earlier.

Level 2.   Safety. An emotional need for security as well as a physical need for shelter. This level follows the first in importance. Modern man creates, builds, or locates a place in which to work, play, live, rest, or sleep where he feels sheltered, safe, and secure from harm while he is vulnerable.

Level 3.   Belonging or Societal. The need to belong and/or identify with a company or a group. For example, being a member of the company's softball team or hunting club is a way of satisfying this need. Membership in a group that has business-building client contact or sales-promotion values is another avenue to the satisfaction of the belonging need.

Level 4.   Esteem or status. This is the ego-satisfaction motivator—the need to enhance one's sense of self-esteem; to

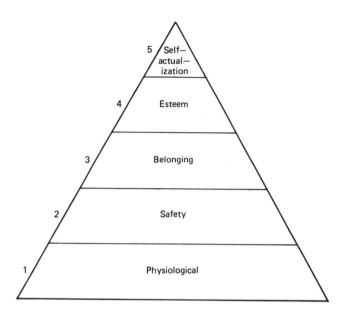

FIGURE 1.   The five levels of needs according to Maslow. Starting at the base of the pyramid, the first two levels represent the "primary" needs, those which we are born with and which do not have to be learned. The remainder are the "secondary" needs and represent those which are learned and acquired throughout our lives by exposure to physical, intellectual, and emotional environments.

gain the respect and admiration of our associates, family, and friends. In its most prevalent form, it is a need for recognition, praise, and congratulations in the presence of others, so that we can be made to appear and feel that we are important individuals. At this level in the hierarchy, we find that the need for power and achievement—and the status derived therefrom—become critical motivators behind individual behavior and performance.

Level 5.   Self-actualization or *Self-fulfillment*. This is a motivator that characterizes many people who start their own businesses, or who strive and drive themselves "up to the top of the ladder of success." The person who is motivated by this need in the Maslow hierarchy is driven to make a reality of the perception he has of himself. The sales executive who envisions himself as president of the corporation or general manager of the division is operating at this level. His "workaholic" behavior may be a reflection of his motivation—the need for self-actualization.

It is quite common that more than one need may be at work at the same time. For example, to reduce it to a thoroughly simplistic level, one can be hungry, thirsty, and sleepy all at the same time, and wonder whether to have a snack before the nap or a nap before the snack. Because one cannot eat, drink, and sleep at the same time, the strongest need will be the one that induces the action. When the strongest need has been satisfied, it will cease to be a motivator and will be replaced by the search and motivation to satisfy another need. This interchange of needs may continue throughout the day—one need in a sort of conflict with another, striving to dominate and become the more powerful motivator.

At a more sophisticated level, one finds the individual coping with survival in the corporate jungle, seeking to satisfy the need for affiliation and identification with the work group. At the next moment, he is attempting to satisfy the need for recognition as an individual achiever. Still higher in the hierarchy is the need for self-actualization; that is, attempting to prove to the board of directors, to one's superiors, and to one's self that one's perception of being the natural leader is realistic and deserves recognition. This recognition can be in the form of a promotion to a job or to a title in the organization that is higher and more powerful than the one now held.

The Hierarchy of Needs is a completely dynamic state of being, always changing, with one need constantly overlapping another throughout the day, week, month, or year—indeed, throughout one's lifetime. This fluency of the motivational needs can be depicted as a vertical bar chart, with one bar for each of the five needs as defined by Maslow. The

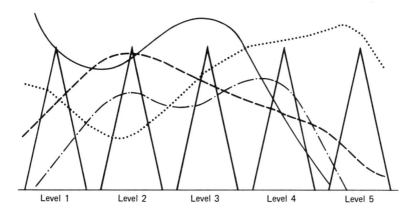

| Level 1 | Level 2 | Level 3 | Level 4 | Level 5 |

FIGURE 2. Maslow's Hierarchy of Needs is a dynamic, continuously changing human activity. The five levels in the hierarchy are shown as individual triangles of equal value. However, the dash, dot, dash-dot, and dash-dash lines graphically depict the fact that, although the needs may be operating simultaneously, they do so at unequal amplitudes. At any one moment, the need with the highest amplitude operates as a dominant motivator.

width of the bars is not important. What is important is that the heights or amplitudes of the bars are in continuous states of fluctuation. The higher the bar, the greater its amplitude, and the more dominant the need is at the moment. This is depicted in Figure 2.

Although we will never know whether these famous scientists could ever have been as effective as you are in meeting a sales quota, the probability is they could identify your people-problems and guide you in a way that could help you develop highly effective solutions. Therefore, a good comprehension of their theories of human behavior can be quite valuable as you attempt to bring order to potentially chaotic situations, provide incentives and motivation, and satisfy your own needs at the same time. After all, the title "manager" does not mean you are not also a human being.

20 MOVING RIGHT ALONG

... With McGregor, McClelland, and Atkinson

There are many behavioral schientists, psychologists, and psychiatrists. Each one has a set of ideas, many of which are built on the basis of observation. Reams and reams of articles and books have been published that are worth reading on your own. However, the purpose of this book is to help you become a more effective practitioner, not a well-educated theorist. Therefore, we will limit this selection of theories to those of three of the more notable scientists: Douglas McGregor, David C. McClelland, and John W. Atkinson. We would be "selling you short" if we did not include them. Their contentions concerning the beliefs and behavior of man under certain sets of conditions are especially important because they are so thoroughly relevant to people who are in managerial positions and in the selling profession, and who, as a result, are continuously confronted with personal relationships and conflicts within the business environment.

McGREGOR—THEORY X AND THEORY Y

The writings of McGregor have often been misunderstood. He did not describe managerial styles. What he did describe were his observations of the theories and beliefs that managers have concerning how people react to work, tasks, and making a living in materialistic societies. McGregor noted that managers have often been slow to use their own knowledge or the available knowledge of the social sciences. He observed that many managers feel that all they have to do is depend on their own rich storehouses of experience, calling on the past to deal with the present and the future. Unfortunately, many managers look down on the theorists in comparing their beliefs with their own, which they feel are based on *reality*. It is strange but true that even those managers who came up through the ranks as engineers and scientists before moving up to managerial levels will often discount the teachings of the theorists. These engineers and scientists-turned-managers started with theory. Different theories were the bases for the fine work they performed, and enabled them to move up to senior levels of management within the organization. How quickly we lose perspective as we climb to higher places!

Without being conscious or aware of it, it is probable that the majority of managers tend to divide their beliefs about human behavior into two categories. These have been labelled by Douglas McGregor as *Theory X* and *Theory Y*. Thus, McGregor contends that managers hold with one of these two beliefs concerning people.

As we pointed out before, it is common to attach labels to people and their roles. It simplifies life to do so because we have also stereotyped many of the roles to which such labels have been attached. The labels "parent," "teacher," "husband," "friend," and "manager" conjure specific images of expected behavior. However, each individual fulfills several roles in rapid, or even simultaneous, sequence. For example, the parent may also have to be a teacher, friend, playmate, arbitrator, protector, and manager. Each of the roles shifts in dominance as the conditions demand. The very same thing is true of the manager. He is the leader of a group of subordinates at one moment and the member of a group of his peers at another. At times he is called upon to be a teacher, decision maker, disciplinarian, trouble shooter, advisor, or observer. In each of these labelled roles the manager's behavior must be modified to suit the situation. Certainly his task is complex, and made more so by the fact that he must adopt different behavioral patterns as he deals with the manager of another department, his immediate superior, or with a superior several levels above him in the organization's structure.

The degree of flexibility of the manager is often related to his concepts of how people respond to their work environments. Few managers are, themselves, consciously aware of the multiple number of roles they are expected to play or fulfill as managers. Thus, the manager and his subordinates may become confused as the roles are changed without explanation or clarification of the elements that are implicit in or that have caused the role to be changed. The manager may be a believer in either of the two theories expounded by McGregor, and he may not even be aware of this belief. Many managers have developed their own styles of management without even being aware of how these styles came into existence. This is especially true of managers whose styles are inflexible. They are always the authoritarian or the benevolent captain of the ship imploring everyone to "pull together, guys!" It is probable that behind every manager's decision or action is an assumption about human nature and behavior.

Theory X: The Traditional Viewpoint

Theory X, or those who believe it describes the behavior of people in the work environment, contends that it is natural for man to avoid work because he has a strong and inherent dislike for it. While man will talk in glowing terms of the "glory of work," he really can't stand the thought of doing it. There are those who go so far as to claim that work is man's punishment for the sins of Adam and Eve in the Garden of Eden, from which they were banished and forced to go out into a world where they had to work in order to survive. The simple statement "a fair day's work for a fair day's pay" may reveal that the person who spoke these words believes, consciously or not, that man has to be rewarded before he will do any work. Theory X holds that, because of this human characteristic of disliking work, most people have to be coerced, bribed, rewarded, and controlled in order to get work done. According to Theory X and those who believe in it, man typically wants to be directed, desires to avoid responsibility, has very little ambition, and wants security but is not willing to work for it—he wants it given to him as his due. Some who adhere to Theory X go so far as to believe that man has to be threatened with punishmnent in order to get him to meet organizational objectives. Is this farfetched? How many times have you heard a sales manager (not you, of course) say: "If you don't (or, if he won't) do such-and-such by this-and-that time, you (he) will be fired!" This manger has usually tried promising material rewards which didn't work and is taking the only route he feels is left—threats of punishment! The sales manager who believes strongly that Theory X is factual and actual may also be heard to say, "You've got to pat them the head while kicking them in the rear!" In its polite form, it is referred to as the "carrot-and-the-stick" approach to motivation. It is this belief that colors and influences the behavior of many sales managers, giving them what is flatteringly called a "style of management."

Knowledge of the social sciences has fortunately been growing during the 20th century. During the first half of the century a belief in Theory X was traditional, However, the capabilities of masses of people, such as the Japanese, to perform good work without apparent external pressure has caused many individuals, managers, and corporations to re-

think their relationships with their employees and their subordinates. Maslow's Hierarchy of Needs is finding greater
acceptance and comprehension among managers at all levels
of an organization as a means for understanding those things
that motivate and underlie human drives. This was discussed
in the previous chapter. Theory X is becoming less popular
as an interpretation of the human side of enterprise.

Theory Y: The Individual and The Group

Theory Y is quite the opposite of Theory X. The central
principle of Theory Y is that members of the organization
can best achieve their own goals by directing their efforts
toward the success of the group or their company. Among
the Japanese, without possibly even being aware of the existence of McGregor, the group is significant while the individual is not. Each member of the group is totally dedicated to
the group; the individual has little thought for his own needs.
Perhaps he has few personal needs. Individual status is not
as important as that of the group to which the individual
belongs and readily identifies himself with. Possibly, one result of the practice of this concept is the high productivity of
the Japanese people. Certainly, it has contributed to the Japanese reputation for high-quality products. We begin to see
a two-way struggle, or a search for answers to questions
about why one national system appears to work better than
another. Is it because, without having declared themselves to
be labelled as such, the Westerner is a believer in Theory X
and the Oriental a believer in Theory Y? The answers to
these questions are not yet known.

What are the assumptions of Theory Y?

1. The expenditure of physical and mental effort in work
    is as natural as play or rest. The average human being
    does not dislike work. Depending upon controllable
    conditions, work may be a source of satisfaction and
    will be performed voluntarily; or, work may be a

source of punishment and punishment will be avoided if possible.

2. External control and the threat of punishment are not the only means for bringing about effort toward organizational objectives. Man will exercise self-direction and self-control in the service of objectives to which he is committed.

3. Commitment to objectives is a function of the rewards associated with their achievement. The most significant of such rewards (e.g., the satisfaction of ego and self-actualization needs) can be direct products of effort directed toward organizational objectives.

4. The average human being learns, under proper conditions, not only to accept but to seek responsibility. Avoidance of responsibility, lack of ambition, and emphasis on security are generally cnsequences of experience, and are not inherent in human characteristics.

5. The capacity to exercise a relatively high degree of imagination, ingenuity, and creativity in the solution of organizational problems is widely, not narrowly, distributed in the population.

6. Under the conditions of modern industrial life, the intellectual potentialities of the average human being are only partially utilized.

Obviously, the two theories are sharply different from each other. This is not as important as the revelation, in Theory Y, that the possibility for human growth and development is strong and inherent, and that the limits of human contribution to the organization's needs are not the limits of human nature, but of the ingenuity of management to discover how to make optimum use of human resources. Theory X is too often used by the inadequate manager to rationalize the failing performance of an individual or of his entire organization. Theory Y dumps the whole thing onto the manager's lap! If his subordinates or employees won't perform, appear

lazy, indifferent, irresponsible, uncreative, and uncoopera-
tive, the implication of Theory Y is that the causes can be
found in management's methods of organization and control.
The sales manager may tend to point the finger at his subordinate managers and the sales people. However, when you
point a finger, be careful; you may glance down to see it
pointing back at you!

McGregor uses an example of a mixture of Theory X and
Theory Y in action. It is especially appropriate to our main
topic, the definition and solution of sales-people problems.
This incident may have a familiar ring; perhaps you can
identify with it personally.

A district manager in a large, geographically decentralized
company is notified that he is being promoted to a policy-
level position at headquarters. It is a big promotion with a
large salary increase. His role in the organization will be a
much more powerful one, and he will be associated with the
major executives of the firm.

The headquarters group who selected him for this position have considered a number of possible candidates. This
man stands out among them in a way which makes him the
natural choice. His performance has been under observation
for some time, and there is little question that he possesses
the necessary qualifications—not only for this opening but
for an even higher position. There is genuine satisfaction that
such an outstanding candidate is available.

The man is appalled. He doesn't want the job. His goal, as
he expresses it, is to be the "best damned district manager in
the company." He enjoys his direct associations with operating people in the field, and he doesn't want a policy-level
job. He and his wife enjoy the kind of life they have created
in a small city, and they both actively dislike the living conditions and social obligations of the headquarters city.

He expresses his feelings as strongly as he can, but his
objections are brushed aside. The organization's needs are
such that his refusal to accept the promotion would be un-
thinkable. His superiors say to themselves that, of course,

when he has settled into the new job, he will recognize that it was the right thing to do. And so he makes the move.

Two years later he is in an even higher position in the company's headquarters organizations, and there is talk that he will probably be the executive vice-president before long. Privately, he indicates that he is considerably unhappy and dissatisfied. He (and his wife) would give anything to be back in the situation he left two years ago.

According to companies engaging in corporate moves, the trend for such movements was down in 1981. The reason may be more related to the economy and cost-reduction programs than to a recognition of the needs of the individual and the practices of McGregor's theories. The preceding story is an example of Theory X in action. Without question, the requirements of the organization are given priority over those of the individual. The needs of the individual, if they are considered at all, are reduced to a belief that material reward and status are all that are essential to satisfy the person. If the district manager really felt so strongly about the move, why did he do it? He had no compelling reason, such as the health of a family member of some severe personal crisis, to fall back on as an overt reason for refusing the promotion.

He was aware, no doubt, and as you have probably seen in your own company or in those of your associates, that to refuse the promotion without excellent reasons would have placed him in jeopardy. He probably would have been considered selfish and childish to have refused such a grand opportunity. Also, it is not likely that he was consulted during the decision-making process concerning the offer of promotion with its requirement to relocate. His personal goals were, most likely, not considered very seriously. The company's goals and the material rewards came first. This unilateral approach to subordinates—excluding them from the internal processes and procedures that have a strong impact on their lives—is a prime example of Theory X in action.

Under the assumptions of Theory Y, the work of the manager is to integrate the needs of his subordinates with the needs of his section, department, division, or company. These are McGregor's words:

> The industrial manager is dealing with adults who are only partially dependent. They can—and will—exercise remarkable ingenuity in defeating the purpose of external controls which they resent. However, they can—and do—learn to exercise self-direction and self-control under appropriate conditions. His task is to help them discover objectives consistent both with organizational requirements and with their own personal goals. And to do so in ways that will encourage genuine commitment to these objectives. Beyond this, his task is to help them achieve these objectives: to act as teacher consultant, colleague, and only rarely as authoritative boss.*

In summary, Theory X is essentially a negative approach to human relations. It assumes that people don't like to work and must be constantly pushed and threatened with loss of security. Theory Y is the positive approach. It presumes that most people who are given meaningful work will try hard to achieve, will provide their own initiative and challenging objectives, and will practice self-control while seeking to attain their objectives. The style that characterizes the individual manager is developed through education, environment, and experience. The style that dominates his behavior is the result of his belief in one or the other of McGregor's two theories—whether or not he has ever heard of McGregor, or of Theory X and Theory Y specifically.

McCLELLAND—POWER, AFFILIATION AND ACHIEVEMENT

David C. McClelland, Professor of Psychology, is one of the leading investigators of motivation and human behavior in

---

* McGregor, *The Human Side of Enterprise*, p. 152.

an achievement-oriented society. His studies have taken him to many countries and to many cultures and ethnic groups. Out of his investigations have come a number of interesting theories. We will discuss those that involve the theory that each of us has three needs: (1) power, (2) affiliation, and (3) achievement. McClelland believes that, with regard to motivation, the only differences from person to person are in the degrees to which these three needs dominate and motivate their behavior at any given moment. His theories seem quite applicable to sales people and, therefore, may help us understand ourselves as managers and potential managers of sales people. They will also enable us to understand the inner "tickings" of the sales people with whom we work and who may some day report to us in the organization.

The Power Need

"Power," in the sense used by McClelland, is not physical strength; nor is it necessarily the kind of power of authority that is inherent in the rank of the individual. It is used in terms of the ability to influence the thoughts and actions of another. The typical example in sales is the "flow of adrenalin" that is discharged into the sales person's system when he learns that he is involved in a competitive selling situation. He learns that a buyer is about to make a selection and issue a substantial purchase order for goods and services. The sales person is determined not to lose this one. (He personally abhors having to write a lost-sale report.) And, taking it almost as a personal challenge to his selling skills, he races out to the buyer's office. With amazing self-control, daring, and skill, he proceeds to persuade the buyer to reconsider his decision. Perhaps he has succeeded in delaying the final decision, thus gaining time for a new "assault." Perhaps he returns with the promise of an order, or with the order itself. Without any doubt he returns with a sense of power. He has won a "battle" against his competitor. He has exercised his power. We have heard sales managers say about some of their top achievers, "Where others get a promise, he gets a deposit; where others get a letter of intent, he gets a firm P.O." Obviously, in such people, the need to exercise power, to be more powerful than their peers and certainly more powerful than their competitors, is strong indeed.

People whose need for power is dominant will often demonstrate this need in meetings and conversations that may originally have been intended for the purpose of creative thought, problem solving, or for the development of group consensus and general agreement. However, the person with a dominant power need has difficulty in "going along with the gang." He must express his individuality and attempt to influence, persuade, or control the thought processes of others in the group. The important thing to this person is not how right he is in his way of thinking. The emphasis is on the satisfaction he gets by successfully persuading others in the group to see things his way.

We can see this need for power as a phenomenon that occurs in a brainstorming session wherein the rules specifically preclude on-the-spot criticism of another's ideas. The person who must satisfy the need for power has great personal difficulty when he is expected to participate in a democratic process. He is perpetually competitive and often overly aggressive. He has a compulsion to impress his ideas on the group or on another individual. At the same time, he will try to put down the ideas of others. Needless to say, this has the potential for creating interpersonal conflicts and frustrations among sales people—individuals in their own right and, perhaps, with power needs of their own—and untidily hands problems to the sales manager that demand wise solutions.

When the sales manager sees these power-need forces at play, he must find a solution that satisfies the needs of each of the individuals, the group, the section, department, division, the company, and, last but not least, his own personal needs as a human being. While the manager has the power that is inherent in his rank and title, this is not necessarily an advantage when the need for power is dominant at the same time in both himself and the individual sales person. The manager may "pull rank." The manager may elect to "give in—just this once!" Neither path is a solution that satisfies both parties. In either response, the manager or the sales person will be frustrated. Several of the case studies given in Chapters 1–18 of this book deal with such situations specifically, and demonstrate ways to deal with such conflicts to assure that nobody loses.

Surely, the need for power is both good and bad at the same time. It is a motivator, but it also involves problems. It is the task of the manager to gain motivational benefits for his group through the appropriate management of the interpersonal conflicts that such needs can generate.

The Affiliation Need

This is a phenomenon experienced by practically every sales manager. Usually, it puzzles and confounds the manager. However, after we review McCelland's definition of the affiliation need I believe we will all have a better understanding of this specific type of behavior. As a direct result, we will also be able to deal more effectively with satisfying the need. Those whose needs are dominated by affiliation derive satisfaction primarily from social and interpersonal activities. They are motivated by a sense of belonging to or identifying with a group or a company. These people will choose friends when offered the choice of working with friends or with highly competent strangers.

One of the characteristics of those whose needs include affiliation is that they invariably become an active part of a group, even joining a clique. They are, at times, compulsive talkers. They make time to become active in the social activities offered by the company, such as the bowling league, softball team, and so on. "Togetherness" is the way they think and conduct themselves. What about the sales man who travels the territory most of the time—out on Monday,

possibly back on Friday or Saturday? He may not have deliberately chosen this type of work assignment; things sometimes just work out that way. He may have as strong a need
for affiliation as the person who primarily works at a desk.

How does he satisfy the need if it is dominant? Think
about the times you wished "Sales man Tom, Dick, or
Harry" would call on some new accounts or take some other
distributor or buyer to lunch for a change—that is, spread his
wings and increase his circle of business contacts. Why does
he repeatedly go out with the same customers? Affiliation!
He can't affiliate with the gang at the office because his "office" is primarily a suitcase and a motel room. He constructs,
without thinking about it, a circle of warm affiliations among
his account people, especially among those who accept him
as "one of us." This strong cultivation of relationships, this
close tie with his accounts, is a valuable and, hopefully,
profitable situation for the company. However, as his manager, you may find yourself hanging onto a hot telephone
with him at the other end of the line sounding off about
the lousy support the home office has been giving to *"my*
customers!"

You have to restrain yourself under these circumstances;
hold back the overwhelming urge to shout back "Who the
heck do you work for, anyway!" You resist the urge and,
after the call is completed and you have started the ball roll-
ing to correct the situation, contemplate for a long moment
the phenomenon that has just manifested itself. Your sales
man is identifying with his customer, not with the company
or with you. He is being very human, which you can't fault
him for. How should you respond? You must find a way that
enables the sales man to continue his relationships. However, perhaps you'd better spend more time with him in the
field, communicate with him more often and with greater
regularity, and bring him into the home office as frequently
as his schedule permits so that he can get to know the people
with whom he interfaces from his remote field locations.
This helps satisfy the dominant need for affiliation, and

helps him identify with you, his home-office associates, and the company—without disconnecting him from his buddies out there in the territory.

The Achievement Need

Reaching their goals and attaining specific and high objectives are among the motivations of sales men with high achievement needs. Money and material rewards are not necessarily among the things that motivate them. However, physical and tangible rewards that are visible to others are viable measurements and indicators of achievement. Many high-achieving sales people obviously have strong dominant needs for achievement. But, have you noted that they are not always turned on by special short-term, big-prize sales contests? This may be due to the fact that the rules of the contest and the awarding of the prizes lack a very important ingredient—*recognition.*

There are personality traits that characterize the person with a dominant need for achievement. They must have immediate feedback; that is, statements of their progress toward their goals. Many sales managers instruct their administrators to send, or even telephone, weekly or daily bookings and shipment reports to their sales people. Many sales managers do not know why this is important. If asked, the answer usually is "Why not? We've always done it this way." Now you know why recognition of achievement is important, why it's so often given this way.

High achievers will generally avoid tasks that are at the extremes of "easy" and "tough." They prefer tasks that are moderately difficult and with at least a 50/50 probability for success. Unlike sales people with dominant needs for affiliation, sales people with dominant needs for achievement are usually loners. They prefer to work independently. Why? Because this enables them to make certain that their performance will be measured and related totally and specifically to their own efforts rather than to someone else's. They avoid risk situations wherein they cannot have control over the outcome. In a card game of poker, they are penny-ante players. They avoid slot machines and gambling tables. They are not excited by a prize that offers them a trip to Las Vegas where gambling is the primary pastime.

It is not unusual to misunderstand the high achiever's rejection of an assignment, especially when one of the newcomers, a "young tiger," eagerly takes up the sword and charges forward. The young tiger may charge, while the high-achieving veteran holds back his enthusiasm for one or more reasons: (1) the young tiger is inexperienced, and is thus unable to evaluate the risks as well as the opportunities built into the task; or (2) his needs are not dominated by achievement, or (3) his needs are for affiliation or power. Unfortunately, to accept enthusiasm as the sole basis for giving or accepting an assignment is to create the potential for a sink-or-swim situation. And, all are involved in the risk, including the manager.

The sales manager must recognize those needs that are dominant in his sales people and direct and control them accordingly. Companies and managers with reputations for people orientation generally attract and support people who are trying to satisfy their needs for affiliation. Hard-nosed managers and organizations generally attract those whose dominant needs are for power. While it is not practicable to make a statement that claims that one type of organization, or the need it attempts to satisfy, is better than another, we can describe the type of organizational environment that attracts and encourages individuals with strong needs for achievement:

1. A reward system. It may include money and material rewards. It must include recognition that is related to the attainment of defined goals.
2. Emphasis on the individual. His performance as a soloist is more important than that of the group.
3. Participative goal setting. People want to share in

the process that determines their quotas and any other quantified goals (including accountable expense budgets).

4. Rapid feedback. People want to know at all times where they stand (they keep records and want to make certain the company's records match theirs), and they expect their rewards to be issued as soon as the task is completed.

5. Independence. Each person wants a direct line of communication with his superior and freedom from having to interact with the entire hierarchy at the home office.

You will note that McClelland deals entirely with motivation and incentive. He pays little, if any, attention to such things as hygiene factors. His theory of power, affiliation, and achievement can be readily identified with Maslow's higher order of learned needs in the Hierarchy of Needs.

ATKINSON—THE DRIVING FORCES OF CONFLICT

John W. Atkinson, Professor of Psychology at the University of Michigan, described an interesting concept of the driving forces produced by "valences." As described earlier by Victor Vroom, a valence is the degree of attractiveness an individual activity or object has as a behavioral goal. It may have positive or negative values as a motivator or, alternatively, as a turn-off. These driving forces can be the cause of personal stress and conflict that can readily affect the on-the-job performance of a sales person. Atkinson defined three basic driving forces containing positive and negative valences that produce internal and personal conflict: (1) *approach/approach,* (2) *avoidance/avoidance,* and (3) *approach/avoidance.* It sounds like scrabble or some other word game. However, it does make sense, as you shall see.

Approach/Approach Conflict

This occurs when a person is attracted to two or more goals that are mutually incompatible from a time or convenience standpoint. Atkinson illustrated this with an example of a child who has to choose between the pleasures of going on a picnic and playing with his friends on the block. We assume that the two *forces* of valence are equal, but necessarily opposite in direction. The child is "torn," so to speak, between two loves. Approach/approach conflicts are relatively easily resolved by any positive influence. A well-spoken word that enhances the attractiveness of one approach over the other, for example, might persuade the child to accept one of the two attractive forces. As the child's resolve toward one of the two approaches increases, the attractiveness of the other approach decreases and the conflict diminishes. When equilibrium exists for the two driving forces of the attractive approach/approach, the equilibrium is quite unstable. It could easily be tilted in one direction or another, upset, broken, or disturbed by a well-timed phrase or by the adding-on of an incentive (a "spiff" of sorts). Because of the instability of the equilibrium of the apppraoch/approach conflict, the time required to reach a decision and resolve the conflict is usually short.

A parallel example in a sales situation is that of the sales person who, in the midst of finalizing a contract with a customer, remembers an invitation to join a group of close friends for cocktails and dinner at the club. Here, he has two attractive situations: (1) bring in an order that is sure to bring recognition from the boss, and (2) enjoy another great evening with the boys. It is late in the day by this time. He believes he can conclude the negotiations with the customer right now and return later in the week for the order. However, he is only "this far away" from getting the order today. For a moment there is a state of equilibrium between the two driving forces. The instability is clear, however, and the

move in the direction of one of the attractions is rapidy resolved when the customer with whom he is negotiating says,
"I think we can wrap this up today, Harry. All I need now is
the signature of the purchasing agent and you can take the
order with you." "How long will it take?" Harry asks.
"About an hour, Harry. Can you wait?" A glance at the
watch and, for a brief moment, Harry almost says "No, I
have to get to a meeting." (The equilibrium is quite upset as
he suddenly moves in the direction of the other force.) However, the wheels turn rapidly in his head and he makes a final
resolution. "Sure," says Harry, "and then how about you
and me going out for a drink and, if you can take the time,
I'd be delighted to have you as my guest for dinner." There
are no losers here.

Avoidance/Avoidance Conflict

Again, Atkinson uses a child's experience as the example. In
this situation, the child is told by a parent to do a chore that
he finds totally disagreeable. He is warned that if he doesn't
do it he will surely be punished. These are two negative
valences. No positive values are present. The child is torn
between two totally disliked forces—an unliked task and an
unwanted punishment. The best thing that can occur here is
for some other happening to come along that can move the
child in a direction that is away from both having to perform
the task and having to face the punishment as an alternative.
Perhaps the child is "saved by the bell;" for example, the
parent suddenly remembers an appointment with a PTA
committee and, because of circumstances, has to take the
child with her. The command to perform the disagreeable
task is canceled, and so is the threat of punishment. While
the child may not find the PTA committee terribly exciting, it
sure is better than the task and beats heck out of the threatened punishment.

Let's examine an example of a sales person who is confronted by the driving forces of an avoidance/avoidance con-

flict. The sales manager has just told the sales person that the marketing manager needs some field intelligence concerning the activities of a competitor in the specific territory, and needs the information by tomorrow. (It is now the end of the fiscal period and the sales forecasts for the next period are due tomorrow.) We all know how sales people hate paperwork and wait until the last minute to do it. The marketing manager's need is genuine. So is the need for the forecast. Conflict! Stress! Emotional confusion! How do we get out of this one? One way is for the sales person to talk with the sales manager about priorities, but then he would have to admit he waited until the very last minute to do his forecasts. This will not sit too well. "Sorry about that!" he can hear the sales manger saying unsympathetically. Another way is to make a judgment and do one or the other. But, he wasn't given this option, was he? Another way is to burn the midnight oil. But he had planned to do this in order to draft the forecasts and then have them typed in the morning for delivery to the boss. Also, he could leave town and chuck it all. This is not very realistic, but awfully tempting. This appears to be an unresolvable dilemma for the sales person, unless something else comes along for which a higher priority can be claimed. To give this story a "happy ending," a very good customer called to say he had just gotten into town and wanted to meet with him "first thing in the morning—and plan to work with me right through lunch."

Approach/Avoidance Conflict

In this positive/negative valence, we have an attraction in conflict with another situation that is unattractive. Again, let's start with a child's experience as an example. The child's little boat is in the ocean a few feet from the shore. The child is driven toward the toy by an obviously positive valence. As the child tries to reach the toy he becomes frightened by the splashing of the waves. He dashes back to shore, only to try again and again, in vain, to retrieve his boat. The two driving forces create a conflict, probably resulting in tears and, probably, a rescue of the little boat by someone else. The conflict is resolved, until the child loses control of the boat once more.

A sales manager may also be confroted by approach/avoidance conflict. He has been invited to a private party which several key accounts will be attending. He has also heard it is to be a "stag" affair with all the trimmings! It all sounds very attractive. But, he has also learned his boss will be there and he knows his boss is very much married and tries to keep his private life separate from his business associates. The boss never goes out socially with his associates. And, he has left no doubt in anyone's mind that he doesn't care to discuss his private affairs.

"What I do is my own business and I'll thank you to keep your nose out of it," has been the clear, although unspoken, message he transmits. And, the sales manager received it loudly and clearly once when he was merely trying to make small talk. Once was enough! Boy, the sales manager would sure like to go to this party. But, if the boss runs into him—and it would be unavoidable at a private party—both would be embarrassed. Perhaps he'd be wise to avoid the party. There'll be another one next year—next year! Oh, well, another night alone with the "tube" won't cause permanent damage, and certainly has less potential for harm than running into the boss "with his hair down."

Wouldn't you have made the same decision?

21 LET'S "CLOSE" ON THIS ONE

When Firing
Is the Final Solution

As has already been said, "Nobody ever told you being a manager was going to be easy!" *And it isn't easy.* But, you've already learned this fact from experience.

You also know that sales people have to keep working at their tasks of selling. Many of the tasks of selling are repetitive—one deals with the same products or services; the same heavy quotas; the same grumpy, hard-headed buyers; the same route; and the same routine. But, the effective sales person learns and benefits from repetition, improving his or her performance each time the task is repeated. He also becomes more familiar with the "buy" signals, thus closing more quickly for bigger dollars. It is, one might conclude, beneficial to the sales person to experience repetition and to view it as a special challenge to his skills.

Of course, repeating one's successes is the ultra-positive view. What about those who repeat their mistakes? In one chapter we discussed and proposed several options that are

251

available to the sales manager for interrupting the cycle of failure that occurs through repetition; that is, doing the same thing, the same way, over and over again—even though it has never worked.

Sales managers are people who manage sales people; only indirectly do they manage sales. The *successful* sales manager learns how to avoid recurring errors or making the same mistakes over and over again. From each experience, he gains knowledge and acquires skills that are transferrable to other situations and people. His skills become flexible and adaptable, enabling him to bring about an effective (i.e., long-term) solution to the inevitable next problem.

And you can be sure there will be a "next problem." We pointed out in the case of Rigid-Roger that there may be some truth to clichés such as "change is our way of life." Creating change, and planning, introducing, implementing, managing, and solving the problems that change can bring with it are part of the manager's task. There is no way that I or anyone else can avoid change. There are only effective/ ineffective or appropriate/inappropriate ways to manage change and those who are affected by it. Controlling the situation and managing the change without getting one's self tangled up in one's own red tape is essential to making change a welcome part of the daily lives of sales people. Yes, properly managed, change can become a welcome event. The secret, if there is only one secret, is in participation. Those who participate in the planning and implementation of change will feel they "own" a piece of the action, and they will be willing, if not eager, to help ensure that the change works beneficially.

We haven't tried to develop a simple definition of the word "manager." The definitions that are regularly offered have, themselves, become unsatisfying clichés. It's too bad about that. In the "Introduction," we do go so far as to offer an answer to the question: "What is a 'successful' manager?" We have provided pragmatic rather than textbook and philosophical discussions that would probably have bored you as much as they would have bored us.

This has been a workbook that contains a series of learning experiences; that is, nonthreatening practice sessions in solving the human side of the equation, as far as sales people are concerned. This human side can and often does tend to interfere with the ability of a high-achieving sales person to maximize his opportunities for achievement. In Chapters 19 and 20, we discussed some of the better-known theories of human behavior and applied them to sales people specifically. Rather than treat the subject as a capsule-course in "how to become a psychologist in a few easy-to-read lessons," we have written in the vernacular of the professional sales person, sales manager, and sales supervisor.

As the sales manager or supervisor, the leader of sales people, the burden falls on you. You cannot escape without sacrificing a significant portion of your effectiveness. Your sales peoples' problems automatically become your problems. Without becoming a religious leader, psychologist, or other type of guru, your task is to lead your people, one at a time if necessary, out of the mess (or mass) of confusion— some of which you may have created yourself. It is your task to maintain productivity, stimulate, and motivate. The successful sales manager is an expert at environmental control— the *work* environment. Motivation cannot exist in a hostile environment; nor does a friendly environment assure motivation. The process is complex because people are complex.

By this time you have learned that you don't solve a people-problem by walking away from it, ignoring it, or by taking a fatal action (firing someone). On the other hand, you don't solve it by charging headlong into it. The constructive solution requires a combination of several vital factors: recognizing that a problem actually does exists; collecting data (acquiring as many *facts* as possible); listing the available alternatives (how many different solutions seem to be open to us); examining the pros and cons of the alternatives; selecting the one alternative that appears to hold the greatest probability for success; gaining agreement that all parties involved will work toward improving the situation; setting benchmarks and programs for measuring progress toward improvement; revising the program and the option, if necessary; and, probably most difficult of all, obtaining an expression of willingness on everyone's part, including yours, to modify personal behavior patterns that may have contributed to the problem in the first place.

We have dealt exclusively with internal situations in this book, and have deliberately avoided how-to-sell anecdotes that often begin with such phrases as "how to turn a 'no' into a 'yes'," "overcoming sales resistance," "closing the tough customers," "cold-call selling," "prospecting for new business," and others with which you are totally familiar. These involve external problems in selling and in managing those who are on the front line every day.

Before any of the external situations can have their "happy endings," the internal ones must have theirs. As a successful sales manager or sales supervisor, you have acquired the knowledge and skills to handle your internal people situations. As a result, you have developed the ability to generate satisfactory solutions to problems. The result is superior performance at all levels. By being successful in sales-people problem solving, you have set the foundations on which to attain the high quotas and bookings in units or dollars by which your own performance is inevitably measured.

WHEN ALL ELSE SEEMS TO FAIL

But, it is true that not all stories will have happy endings. Try as we might to avoid and evade failure, nobody's perfect. The best laid plans can turn into disasters because of the sheer, utter complexity of people. Suppose, despite your best shot, that one of your real-life case studies just doesn't seem to be working out. What can you do when all else fails? There are several approaches to this problem. One is the *defensive* approach, which many Personnel Department managers prescribe from the first day the people-problem is recognized. Another is the *self-sacrificing* approach which some sales-people managers adopt.

In the defensive approach, the sales manager is urged to keep a detailed log (times, dates, and places) of all contacts (discussions, responses, promises, commitments, actions, and warnings) that have occurred between himself and his "problem child." Then, when all else fails—*zap*—fire the guy! You tried your best and nobody will fault you. Want to bet on this?

In the self-sacrificing approach, you "learn to live with the bomb!" You put up with, cover up, or explain away the situation. You become a one-man demolition squad, hoping to defuse the whole affair. However, to carry this analogy a bit further, what does a member of a demolition squad do with a defused bomb? He takes it out in the field and detonates it. Even a defused bomb is dangerous; you can't live with it by any means.

There must be another way. (Sorry, but there is no easy or quick way, but there is an appropriate compromise.) You have the responsibility to make certain, beyond the shadow of a doubt, that you did everything possible to bring about a satisfactory solution through the means of behavior modification (your own as well as that of the problem child).

Our suggestion is to follow the recommendation of the Personnel Department. Keep a log, but not for defensive purposes. Keep it for evaluative purposes. Keep it to enable you to accurately review the problem and your own handling of it. Keep it as a personal diary of your experiences as a manager, as a book of knowledge based on actual practice in real life. If heaven forbids, it is necessary for you to provide legal or political evidence of how you handled the situation (which is most likely where the Personnel Department is coming from), your diary will serve the purpose. However, treat it as a personal textbook, rather than something to be used as a potential defense.

What about "living with the bomb?" During the period that runs from *discovery of problem to control of problem*, you will have to live with this bomb. However, none of us can live with it forever. The stress such an experience would place on us would be much too much if it had no ending.

If all else seems to be failing, don't try to go it all alone. Take your diary to your supervisor. Make certain the whole situation isn't a big surprise to him. As a prudent person, you have probably been keeping him posted and aware of your progress in handling the affair all along. When the time comes to admit that the situation can't be corrected—not that you have failed, as the diary will reveal—make certain you have your supervisor's support. He may very well provide another valuable perspective. Through a constructive interchange of observations and ideas, it is possible that a new approach, one that hasn't been considered or tried, may evolve. It is not unusual for someone who is not quite so close to the forest to see a special something about this one bothersome "tree." Perhaps the solution is a temporary reassignment for the sales person to another job. An inside assignment with a series of useful tasks may produce a constructive change in the environment while enabling productive and satisfying work to be accomplished. In due course, the sales person may help resolve the original problem and may eagerly return to his sales spot with batteries fully recharged—and with a newly discovered, more positive perspective.

Reality and experience tell and show us that, although you may have mastered the theories of personality growth and are competent in applying the behavioral sciences to the management of your sales group and individuals, *firing* a problem employee may eventually be the only valid solution.

Firing may be justified in a situation that involves a sales person who doesn't respond cooperatively and constructively to any of the tried-and-true courses of action. In fact, he may respond with intensified hostility and a level of conflict that go beyond sense and logic. Yes, you may have to reach the conclusion that *when all else has failed*, despite your sincere and intelligent efforts, firing may be the only solution that assures the continued growth and prosperity of the sales office, district, region, department, and company. Get on with it! And then, move along to the next stage as you continue to be a successful problem-solver and an effective manager of sales people.